Wonderful ways to prepare

MICROWAVE DISHES

by JO ANN SHIRLEY

TITLES AVAILABLE

Wonderful Ways to Prepare
HORS D'OEUVRES & FIRST COURSES
SOUPS
MEAT
FISH & SEAFOOD
STEWS & CASSEROLES
SALADS
DESSERTS
CAKES & COOKIES
BARBECUES
ITALIAN FOOD
CHINESE DISHES
CROCKERY POT DISHES
FOOD FOR FREEZING
PRESERVES
VEGETARIAN DISHES
CALORIE CONTROLLED DISHES
CHEESECAKES
COCKTAILS & MIXED DRINKS
CHICKEN
MEALS IN A WOK
MICROWAVE DISHES
EGGS
PRESSURE COOKER DISHES
ASIAN MEALS
BISCUITS AND COOKIES
CAKES AND SWEETS
CREPES & PANCAKES
BLENDER & MIXER DISHES
FONDUES

Wonderful ways to prepare

MICROWAVE DISHES

PUBLISHED BY
PLAYMORE INC. New York, USA
AND WALDMAN PUBLISHING CORP. New York, USA

AYERS & JAMES
CROWS NEST AUSTRALIA

PUBLISHED BY
PLAYMORE INC. New York, USA
AND WALDMAN PUBLISHING CORP. New York, USA

PUBLISHED IN AUSTRALIA
BY AYERS & JAMES
CROWS NEST. AUSTRALIA

COPYRIGHT 1983
AYERS & JAMES PTY. LTD.
5 ALEXANDER STREET
CROWS NEST N.S.W. AUSTRALIA

Printed in Canada/Cover Printed in USA

ISBN 0 86908-232 9

Contents

Appetizers

Stuffed Vine Leaves

1 lb (500 g) can vine leaves
½ cup raisins
2 tablespoons olive oil
2 small onions, minced
1 clove garlic, minced
1 cup white rice
2 cups (500 ml) chicken stock
⅔ cup pine nuts

¼ cup minced parsley
¾ teaspoon salt
¼ teaspoon black pepper
½ teaspoon nutmeg
1 large tomato, peeled and chopped
¼ cup (65 ml) lemon juice
water

1. Rinse the vine leaves under cold water and drain well.
2. Pour enough water on the raisins to cover. Set aside for at least ½ hour. Drain.
3. Pour the oil into a ceramic or glass casserole dish and heat in the microwave oven on the highest setting for two minutes.
4. Add the onions and garlic and cook for another minute.
5. Stir in the rice until well-coated with the oil. Cook for two minutes.
6. Add the chicken stock, drained raisins and pine nuts. Cover and cook for ten minutes.
7. Remove from the oven and uncover. Allow to stand for 15 minutes.
8. Stir in the parsley, salt, pepper, nutmeg and tomato.
9. Put a spoonful of the mixture onto each of the vine leaves and roll up.
10. Put the stuffed vine leaves on a shallow glass baking dish in layers with unfilled vine leaves inbetween.
11. Pour on enough water to cover. Sprinkle on the lemon juice.
12. Cover with paper and cook for 15 minutes at the highest setting. Cool in the liquid then drain and chill.

Serves 4-6.

Chicken-Pork Terrine

2 lb (1 kg) cooked chicken meat
1½ lb (750 g) pork sausage meat
¼ lb (125 g) ham, diced
½ cup minced scallions
2 cloves garlic, minced
2 eggs, beaten
1 teaspoon tarragon
½ teaspoon basil

2 tablespoons minced parsley
¼ cup (65 ml) dry sherry
1 teaspoon salt
½ teaspoon black pepper
½ cup (125 g) soft butter
¾ lb (375 g) bacon
toast

1. Dice the chicken and set aside.
2. Line a glass or ceramic loaf tin with half the bacon.
3. Mix together all the ingredients except the chicken and bacon. Blend thoroughly.
4. Spread one third of the sausage mixture over the bacon. Top with half the diced chicken then another third of the sausage meat. Then spread on the rest of the chicken and the last third of the sausage mixture. Lay the remaining bacon on top.
5. Cook in the microwave oven on the highest setting for 20 minutes. Turn the dish around half-way through the cooking time.
6. Remove the terrine from the oven and cool. Put weights on top of the terrine (cans of food are good weights) and put in the refrigerator for at least 24 hours before serving. Serve with warm toast.

Serves 6-8.

Spicy Meatballs

1 lb (500 g) ground lean beef
1 teaspoon salt
½ teaspoon black pepper
2 teaspoons soy sauce
1 egg, lightly beaten
1 clove garlic, minced

1 small onion, minced
⅓ cup dried bread crumbs
¼ cup (65 ml) cream
1 teaspoon (or more to taste) Tabasco sauce
1 tablespoon vegetable oil

1. Thoroughly blend all the ingredients except the oil.
2. Form into small meatballs.
3. Pour the oil onto a ceramic or glass plate and heat in the microwave oven for 15 seconds.
4. Place the meatballs on the plate (no more than ten at a time) and cook on the highest setting for two minutes. Turn over half-way through the cooking time.
5. Serve with toothpicks.

Serves 4-6.

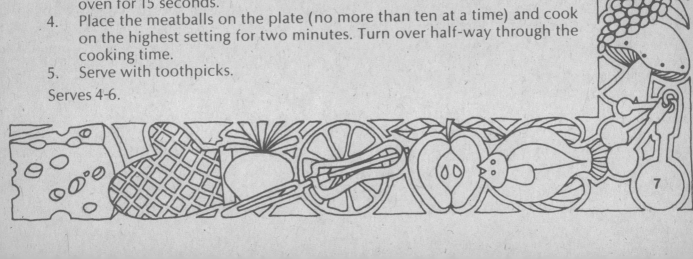

Shrimp with Herbs

1½ lb (750 g) raw shrimp
1½ tablespoons olive oil
¼ cup minced scallions
1 clove garlic, minced
2 teaspoons chopped fresh tarragon

2 tablespoons minced parsley
1 tablespoon minced chives
2 teaspoons minced fresh basil
½ cup (125 ml) white vermouth
salt and pepper

1. Peel and de-vein the shrimp but leave the tails on.
2. Pour the oil onto a ceramic or glass plate and add the scallions, garlic, tarragon, parsley, chives, basil and vermouth. Cook for one minute in the microwave oven at the highest setting.
3. Put the shrimp on the plate coating with the herbs. Cook for three minutes on the highest setting, turning once during the cooking time.
4. Season with salt and pepper and serve immediately.

Serves 4-6.

Plain Shrimp

1½ lb (750 g) raw large shrimp
¼ cup (65 ml) olive oil
salt

1. Pour the oil onto a shallow glass or ceramic dish. Heat the oil in the microwave oven for one minute on the highest setting.
2. Place the shrimp on the dish and cook for three minutes turning once during the cooking time.
3. Sprinkle salt generously on the shrimp and serve. (It's a good idea to give the guests fingerbowls with this dish!)

Serves 4-6.

Garlic Shrimp

1½ lb (750 g) raw shrimp
5 cloves garlic, peeled and sliced
½ cup (125 ml) olive oil
1½ tablespoons lemon juice
¾ teaspoon tarragon

1. Peel and de-vein the shrimp.
2. Put the shrimp in a shallow glass or ceramic dish.
3. Mix together the garlic, olive oil, lemon juice and tarragon. Pour over the shrimp.
4. Cook in the microwave oven at the highest setting for eight minutes. Turn the shrimp around half-way through the cooking time.
5. Serve hot with toothpicks.

Serves 4-6.

Cheese Fondue

½ lb (250 g) cream cheese
1 clove garlic, minced
1¼ cups (300 ml) milk
½ cup grated Swiss cheese

1 cup grated Parmesan cheese
½ teaspoon salt
¼ teaspoon white pepper
French bread, cut into cubes

1. Put the cream cheese and garlic into a ceramic fondue dish. Cook in the microwave oven on the highest setting for about two minutes.
2. Remove from the oven and stir in the milk until smooth.
3. Add the Swiss cheese and Parmesan cheese and return to the oven. Cook, uncovered for about four minutes or until cheese melts. Stir a couple of times during the cooking time.
4. Add the salt and pepper. If too thick add a little more milk.
5. Serve with French bread cubes.

Serves 4-6.

Spicy Cheese Dip

2 tablespoons vegetable oil
2 medium onions, minced
1½ tablespoons all-purpose flour
½ cup (125 ml) chicken stock
½ cup (125 g) sour cream

⅔ cup minced sweet green pepper
minced hot chilies to taste
2½ cups grated cheese
crackers

1. Pour the oil in a ceramic serving dish and heat in the microwave oven on the highest setting for one minute.
2. Stir in the onions and return to the oven for about three minutes or until soft. Stir a few times during the cooking time.
3. Sprinkle on the flour and stir to blend.
4. Slowly add the chicken stock, then the sour cream.
5. Cook for one minute.
6. Add the green pepper, chilies and cheese. Mix thoroughly and stir until the cheese is melted. If the mixture cools, return to the oven for one minute or until the cheese melts.
7. Serve with crackers.

Serves 6-8.

Mushrooms with Herbs

1 lb (500 g) fresh mushrooms
   (uniform in size)
2 tablespoons (40 g) butter
1 small onion, minced
1 clove garlic, minced
1 teaspoon oregano
1 tablespoon minced fresh basil

2 tablespoons minced parsley
2 tablespoons minced chives
1 teaspoon fresh minced
   rosemary
2 tablespoons lemon juice
2 tablespoons dry sherry

1. Wipe the mushrooms with a damp cloth. Remove and discard the stems.
2. Melt the butter in a ceramic dish in the microwave oven at the highest setting.
3. Add the onion, garlic, oregano, basil, parsley, chives and rosemary. Cook for one minute in the oven.
4. Add the lemon juice, sherry and mushrooms. Mix well to ensure that the mushrooms are well-coated.
5. Cook in the oven for about six minutes, stirring frequently.
6. Serve warm with toothpicks.

Serves 6.

Creamed Mushrooms

1 lb (500 g) fresh mushrooms
salt
freshly ground black pepper
1½ cups (375 ml) cream
2 tablespoons dry sherry
toast

1. Wipe the mushrooms with a damp cloth then slice thinly.
2. Put the mushrooms into a glass or ceramic baking dish and sprinkle with salt and pepper to taste.
3. Mix together the cream and sherry. Pour over the mushrooms and blend thoroughly.
4. Cook in the microwave oven for about 15 minutes, stirring frequently.
5. Serve on top of hot toast.

Serves 6.

Almond Shrimp

⅓ cup (85 g) butter
2 cloves garlic, minced
2 tablespoons grated onions
⅔ cup slivered almonds
1½ lb (750 g) shelled raw shrimp
minced parsley

1. Melt the butter in a glass or ceramic baking dish in the microwave oven on the highest setting.
2. Add the garlic, onions and almonds and cook for one minute.
3. De-vein the shrimp and add to the almonds stirring well to ensure that the shrimp are well-coated.
4. Cook for about five minutes or until the shrimp have turned pink.
5. Sprinkle on the parsley and serve with toothpicks.

Serves 6.

Stuffed Mushrooms

24 large fresh mushrooms
¼ lb (125 g) shelled shrimp
¼ cup water chestnuts, minced
½ lb (250 g) ground pork
¼ cup minced ham
1 clove garlic, minced

¼ teaspoon grated fresh ginger
1½ tablespoons cornstarch
½ teaspoon brown sugar
1½ tablespoons soy sauce
minced parsley

1. Wipe the mushrooms with a damp cloth and remove the stems.
2. De-vein the shrimp and mix with the chestnuts, pork, ham, garlic and ginger.
3. Sprinkle on the cornstarch, sugar and soy sauce and blend thoroughly.
4. Fill each mushroom cap with the mixture and place on a glass or ceramic baking dish.
5. Cover and cook in the microwave oven on the highest setting for about ten minutes.
6. Sprinkle with minced parsley and serve hot.

Serves 4-6.

Artichoke Squares

1 lb (500 g) can artichoke hearts
½ cup chopped onions
1 clove garlic, minced
5 eggs, beaten
⅓ cup bread crumbs
½ teaspoon salt

¼ teaspoon black pepper
¼ teaspoon Tabasco sauce
1½ cups grated Cheddar cheese
⅔ cup grated Parmesan cheese
⅓ cup minced parsley

1. Drain the artichokes and pour enough of the liquid into a glass or ceramic baking dish to cover the bottom. Chop the artichoke hearts and set aside.
2. Put the onions and garlic into the baking dish and cook in the microwave oven on the highest setting for about three minutes or until the onions are soft.
3. Mix the eggs with the bread crumbs, salt, pepper, Tabasco sauce, cheeses, parsley and chopped artichoke hearts. Pour over the onion mixture.
4. Cook in the oven for about ten minutes or until set. Remove from oven and allow to sit for about ten minutes before cutting into squares.

Serves 6.

Chicken Liver Pate

¾ cup (185 g) butter
2 cloves garlic, minced
¼ cup minced onion
1 lb (500 g) chicken livers
⅓ cup (85 ml) dry sherry
¼ teaspoon paprika

1 teaspoon salt
½ teaspoon black pepper
1 hard-boiled egg, minced
fingers of toast
minced chives

1. Melt the butter in a glass baking dish in the microwave oven on the highest setting.
2. Add the garlic and onion and cook for 30 seconds.
3. Stir in the chicken livers, cover and cook for about four minutes or until just tender. Stir a couple of times during the cooking time.
4. Pour the sherry into an electric blender with the paprika, salt and pepper. Add the chicken liver mixture and whirl until smooth.
5. Add the hard-boiled egg and pour the mixture into a dish. Cover and chill for several hours or overnight.
6. Spread onto the toast and sprinkle with chives.

Serves 6-8.

Anchovy Dip

½ cup (125 g) butter
3 tablespoons olive oil
3 garlic cloves, minced
½ cup minced onions
6 anchovy fillets, drained
potato chips or crackers

1. Mix together the butter, olive oil, garlic and onions in a glass or ceramic serving bowl.
2. Mince the anchovy fillets and stir into the butter mixture.
3. Cook in the microwave oven for about one minute or until the butter melts.
4. Mix well and serve with potato chips or crackers.

Serves 4-6.

Savory Meatballs

½ lb (250 g) pork sausage meat
¾ lb (375 g) ground beef
½ teaspoon salt
½ teaspoon powdered mustard
½ teaspoon nutmeg
1 clove garlic, minced

1 large egg, beaten
⅓ cup dried bread crumbs
⅓ cup minced scallions
1 tablespoon minced parsley
tomato sauce
German mustard

1. Mix together all the ingredients except tomato sauce and German mustard.
2. Form into small meatballs and put on a shallow glass baking dish in a single layer.
3. Bake in the microwave oven on the highest setting, covered, for about five minutes. Turn the meatballs during the cooking time.
4. Serve the meatballs warm with tomato sauce and mustard.

Serves 6.

Beef Squares

1 lb (500 g) rump steak, weighed
  without fat
½ cup (125 ml) dry white wine
2 tablespoons vegetable oil
1½ tablespoons soy sauce

2 cloves garlic, minced
1 teaspoon grated fresh ginger
½ teaspoon powdered mustard
2 tablespoons black peppercorns
2 tablespoons vegetable oil

1. Cut the steak into bite-size cubes.
2. Mix together the wine, two tablespoons vegetable oil, soy sauce, garlic, ginger and mustard.
3. Add the steak and mix well to ensure that each piece is well-coated. Set aside and allow to marinate for several hours. Drain and pat dry.
4. Slightly crush the peppercorns and press onto the steak cubes.
5. Pour the second two tablespoons of oil onto a glass baking dish and heat in the microwave oven on the highest setting for one minute.
6. Put the beef cubes in the dish in a single layer. Cook for four minutes or until the cubes are cooked. Turn over during the cooking time.
7. Serve warm with toothpicks.

Serves 6-8.

Scallops

1 lb (500 g) scallops, halved
1 teaspoon sugar
⅓ cup (85 ml) lemon juice
salt and pepper

1. Mix the scallops with the sugar and lemon juice.
2. Place on a glass baking dish and cook in the microwave oven on the highest setting for two minutes. Stir a couple of times during the cooking time.
3. Remove from oven, season with salt and pepper and serve with toothpicks.

Serves 6.

Country Paté

½ lb (250 g) ground pork
1 lb (500 g) ground veal
1 lb (500 g) ground lambs liver
2 cloves garlic, minced
1 teaspoon thyme
¼ teaspoon nutmeg
1 teaspoon salt

½ teaspoon black pepper
2 tablespoons brandy
2 tablespoons dry sherry
1 hard-boiled egg, minced
½ cup (125 ml) cream
2 eggs, beaten
bacon

1. Combine all the ingredients except the bacon. Mix only until just blended.
2. Put into a glass loaf dish.
3. Put bacon on the top overlapping the edges.
4. Cook in the microwave oven for about 25 minutes, turning the dish around half-way through the cooking time.
5. Remove the dish and place weights (cans of food are good weights) on the top to consolidate the paté. Chill for at least 24 hours before serving.
6. Serve with hot toast.

Serves 6.

Desserts, Cakes and Cookies

Raspberry Cake

3 cups fresh raspberries	2 cups all-purpose flour
all-purpose flour	2½ teaspoons baking powder
½ cup (125 g) butter	¼ teaspoon salt
1¼ cups sugar	⅔ cup (165 ml) milk
1 teaspoon cinnamon	1 teaspoon vanilla
3 eggs	whipped cream

1. Dust the raspberries with the flour ensuring they are thoroughly coated. Shake off excess flour.
2. Cream together the butter, sugar and cinnamon until smooth and creamy.
3. Add the eggs one at a time, beating well after each addition.
4. Add the flour with the baking powder and salt alternately with the milk and vanilla.
5. Butter and flour an 8-inch (20-cm) glass or ceramic baking dish. Pour one-third of the cake mix into the dish. Spoon on half the raspberries, pour on another third of the cake mix, the rest of the raspberries then the remaining cake batter. Cook in the microwave oven on the highest setting for ten minutes or until the cake is done, rotating the dish several times during the cooking period. Serve with lots of whipped cream.

Banana-Nut Cake

½ cup (125 g) butter
¾ cup brown sugar
⅔ cup mashed bananas
1½ teaspoons lemon juice
1 teaspoon grated lemon rind
2 eggs, lightly beaten

1¼ cups all-purpose flour
½ teaspoon baking powder
½ teaspoon baking soda
½ teaspoon salt
½ teaspoon cinnamon
⅔ cup chopped walnuts

1. Cream together the butter and sugar until light and fluffy.
2. Add the bananas, lemon juice, grated lemon rind and eggs. Beat well.
3. Sift together the flour, baking powder, baking soda, salt and cinnamon.
4. Stir the sifted ingredients into the banana mixture with the walnuts. Mix until just combined.
5. Butter and flour a square glass or ceramic baking dish, then line with wax paper.
6. Pour the cake mixture into the dish and cook in the microwave oven on the highest setting for eight minutes. Rotate the dish a quarter of a turn every two minutes. Remove from the oven and allow to stand in the dish for five minutes. Remove from the dish and cool for ten minutes before removing the paper and serving.

Coffee Cake

1½ cups all-purpose flour
1½ teaspoons baking powder
½ teaspoon salt
⅓ cup (85 g) butter
¾ cup sugar
1 egg, lightly beaten
½ cup (125 ml) milk

1¼ teaspoons vanilla
2 tablespoons all-purpose flour
1 tablespoon confectioners' sugar
1 tablespoon brown sugar
½ teaspoon cinnamon
2½ tablespoons (50 g) butter
2 tablespoons chopped nuts

1. Sift the flour with the baking powder and salt. Set aside.
2. Cream together the butter and sugar until light and fluffy.
3. Add the egg and beat well.
4. Add the sifted dry ingredients to the butter and sugar mixture alternately with the milk and vanilla. The mixture will be somewhat stiff.
5. Spoon the mixture into an 8-inch (20-cm) glass or ceramic baking dish which has been buttered and floured.
6. Combine the two tablespoons of flour with the confectioners' sugar, brown sugar, cinnamon, butter and nuts. Sprinkle on top of the cake mixture and cook in the microwave oven on the highest setting for about five minutes or until the cake is done. Rotate the dish a couple of times during the cooking period.

Graham Cracker Cake

3 eggs, separated	2¼ cups graham cracker crumbs
¾ cup white sugar	⅛ teaspoon salt
¼ cup brown sugar	1 teaspoon cinnamon
½ cup (125 g) butter	1¼ teaspoons baking powder
¾ cup (185 ml) milk	fresh peach slices
1¼ teaspoons vanilla	whipped cream

1. Beat the egg whites until foamy. Continue beating, gradually adding ¼ cup of the white sugar, until the egg whites are stiff. Set aside.
2. Cream the butter with the rest of the white sugar and the brown sugar until light and fluffy.
3. Add the egg yolks, milk and vanilla, beating well.
4. Stir in the cracker crumbs, salt, cinnamon and baking powder.
5. Fold in the beaten egg whites.
6. Butter an 8-inch (20-cm) glass or ceramic baking dish and line it with wax paper. Pour the cake mixture into the dish and cook in the microwave oven for ten minutes or until the cake is done. Rotate the dish several times during the cooking period. Leave the cake in the dish for about ten minutes before turning it out to cool on a wire rack. Serve with fresh peaches and whipped cream.

Health Bar

3 tablespoons sesame seeds	½ cup chopped almonds
½ cup (125 ml) honey	⅓ cup chopped dried apricots
¾ cup (185 g) peanut butter	⅓ cup chopped dried apples
2 tablespoons chopped walnuts	2 tablespoons wheatgerm
3 cups muesli	¼ cup flaked coconut

1. Spread the sesame seeds on a shallow glass or ceramic baking dish and toast in the microwave oven on the highest setting.
2. Pour the honey into a large glass mixing bowl and heat to the boiling point in the microwave oven.
3. Add the peanut butter and chopped walnuts and cook for ½ minute.
4. In another bowl combine the muesli, chopped almonds, apricots, apples, wheatgerm, coconut and toasted sesame seeds.
5. Pour on the hot honey mixture and blend thoroughly.
6. Press the mixture into a well-buttered shallow glass or ceramic baking dish. Cook for one minute in the oven. Press down again, cover and cool for a couple of hours before cutting into bars.

Date Pudding

1 cup (250 ml) water
¾ cup chopped dates
1 teaspoon baking soda
1½ cups all-purpose flour
¾ cup chopped walnuts
½ teaspoon baking powder
¼ teaspoon salt
⅓ cup (85 g) butter
1¼ cups sugar

2 eggs
1½ teaspoons grated lemon rind
1 teaspoon cinnamon
¼ teaspoon nutmeg
1½ tablespoons lemon juice
whipped cream
candied orange and lemon peel
slivered almonds

1. Put the water in a small bowl and heat to the boiling point in the microwave oven on the highest setting. Stir in the dates and baking soda and set aside.
2. Mix together the flour, walnuts, baking powder and salt and set aside.
3. With an electric mixer, beat together the butter and sugar.
4. Add the eggs, one at a time, then the grated lemon rind, cinnamon, nutmeg and lemon juice.
5. Gradually add the flour mixture, then the dates with the water.
6. Spoon the pudding into a square glass or ceramic baking dish and cook in the microwave oven on the highest setting for ten minutes rotating the dish a quarter of a turn every two minutes. Cool in the dish.
7. Serve with whipped cream, mixed peel and almonds.

Serves 8.

Pumpkin Pudding

3 eggs, lightly beaten
¼ teaspoon salt
⅓ cup (85 ml) maple syrup
1 cup mashed cooked pumpkin
½ teaspoon cinnamon

¼ teaspoon nutmeg
¾ cup (185 ml) evaporated milk
¼ cup raisins
whipped cream
nutmeg

1. Beat the eggs with the salt and maple syrup.
2. Add the pumpkin, cinnamon, nutmeg and evaporated milk.
3. Fold in the raisins.
4. Pour the mixture into individual glass or ceramic dessert dishes.
5. Cook in the microwave oven on the highest setting for about four minutes or until set.
6. Serve the pudding chilled garnished with whipped cream and sprinkled with a little nutmeg.

Chocolate Brownies

¼ lb (125 g) cooking chocolate
½ cup (125 g) butter
2 eggs
1 cup sugar
1 cup all-purpose flour

½ teaspoon salt
½ teaspoon baking powder
1¼ teaspoons vanilla
1 cup coarsely chopped walnuts

1. Line a square glass or ceramic baking dish with wax paper, then butter the paper.
2. Put the chocolate and butter into a glass bowl and heat in the microwave oven on the highest setting for about one minute or until the chocolate is completely melted.
3. Blend the eggs with the sugar. Beat well.
4. Sift together the flour, salt and baking powder, then add to the egg and sugar mixture.
5. Stir in the vanilla, chopped walnuts and the chocolate mixture.
6. Spread into the lined baking dish. Cook in the microwave oven for five minutes. Remove from the oven and cool in the dish. Remove the paper and cut into squares.

Apple Flan

¼ cup (65 g) butter
½ cup sugar
2 egg yolks
1 teaspoon vanilla

1 cup all-purpose flour
5 large cooking apples
¼ cup apricot jam
1 teaspoon grated orange rind

1. Mix together the butter, half the sugar and the egg yolks. Beat until smooth.
2. Add the vanilla and the flour, a little at a time, and mix to a smooth dough. Roll out to fit a glass or ceramic pie dish. Prick the bottom with a fork and cook in the microwave oven on the highest setting for 6-7 minutes.
3. Peel, core and slice the apples and arrange on the cooked pastry. Sprinkle with the remaining sugar. Cook in the oven for about six minutes or until the apples are soft.
4. Heat the apricot jam with the orange rind in a glass bowl in the oven. Brush onto the flan while it is still warm. Serve warm or chilled.

Serves 6.

Lemon Flan

Pastry:
1¼ cups all-purpose flour
pinch of salt
½ cup (125 g) butter
cold water

Filling:
¾ cup cornstarch
1½ cups sugar

2½ cups (625 ml) water
5 egg yolks
⅔ cup (165 ml) lemon juice
1 tablespoon grated lemon rind

Topping:
whipped cream
slivered almonds

1. Sift the flour with the salt into a mixing bowl. Add the butter and mix until it has the consistency of bread crumbs. Add just enough cold water to form a firm dough. Roll out the dough to fit a 10-inch (25-cm) glass or ceramic pie dish. Prick the bottom of the pastry with a fork. Cook in the microwave oven on the highest setting for about eight minutes, rotating the dish a quarter of a turn half-way through the cooking time.
2. Mix together the cornstarch, sugar and water in a glass mixing bowl. Cook in the oven for two minutes, stirring a couple of times.
3. Lightly beat the egg yolks and add to the cornstarch mixture with the lemon juice and lemon rind. Pour into the prepared pastry and cook in the oven for five minutes. Remove from the oven and chill.
4. Serve the flan topped with whipped cream and almonds.

Serves 8.

Baked Apples

4 large cooking apples
1 tablespoon raisins
1 tablespoon candied orange and
  lemon peel
1 tablespoon chopped dates

1 tablespoon chopped glacé
  cherries
⅓ cup chopped walnuts
1 teaspoon cinnamon
⅓ cup (85 ml) maple syrup

1. Core the apples and remove some of the peel around the top.
2. Mix together the raisins and mixed peel in a small glass bowl. Cover with water and cook in the microwave oven on the highest setting for one minute. Drain.
3. Mix the raisins and peel with the dates, cherries, walnuts and cinnamon. Fill the apple cores with this mixture and place on a shallow glass or ceramic baking dish.
4. Pour the maple syrup over the apples and cover with plastic wrap. Cook in the oven for 7-8 minutes. Serve warm.

Serves 4.

Peaches in Wine

2 cups (500 ml) red wine
¾ cup sugar
¼ teaspoon nutmeg
½ teaspoon cinnamon

1 teaspoon grated lemon rind
1 teaspoon grated orange rind
6 fresh peaches
whipped cream

1. Mix together the red wine, sugar, nutmeg, cinnamon, lemon and orange rind in a glass or ceramic baking dish. Cook in the microwave oven on the highest setting until it reaches the boiling point. Stir several times during this period.
2. Peel the peaches and place in the baking dish. Cook for 5-6 minutes, basting often with the syrup.
3. Allow the peaches to cool in the syrup, basting often.
4. Serve at room temperature or chilled with plenty of whipped cream.

Serves 6.

Chocolate Pudding

½ lb (250 g) milk chocolate
⅔ cup sugar
2½ tablespoons cornstarch
2½ cups (625 ml) milk

1 cup (250 ml) cream
4 eggs, lightly beaten
1¼ teaspoons vanilla
grated dark chocolate

1. Melt the chocolate in the microwave oven on the highest setting.
2. Mix together the sugar, cornstarch, milk and cream in a glass or ceramic bowl. Put into the oven and cook for two minutes.
3. Add the chocolate and eggs. Mix well and cook for four minutes, stirring several times.
4. Add the vanilla and cool. Chill for several hours before serving garnished with grated chocolate.

Serves 6.

Oranges with Cointreau

4 **large oranges**
¾ **cup sugar**
¾ **cup (185 ml) water**
¼ **teaspoon cinnamon**
¼ **cup (65 ml) Cointreau**

1. Peel the oranges. Remove the pith from the peel and cut the peel of two of the oranges into thin slices.
2. Mix together the sugar, water, cinnamon and orange peel in a large glass or ceramic mixing bowl. Cook in the microwave oven on the highest setting for five minutes stirring a few times.
3. Add the Cointreau and the oranges. Spoon the syrup over the oranges frequently while the syrup cools. Serve the oranges at room temperature or chilled. (Delicious with lashings of whipped cream.)

Serves 4.

Pineapple Upside-Down Pudding

2 **16 oz cans pineapple slices**
2 **tablespoons (40 g) butter**
2 **tablespoons maple syrup**
¾ **cup (185 g) butter**

1 **cup brown sugar**
3 **eggs, lightly beaten**
3 **cups cake flour**
3 **teaspoons baking powder**
½ **teaspoon cinnamon**

1. Drain the pineapples and reserve the liquid.
2. Butter a large glass bowl and spread the maple syrup over the butter.
3. Place pineapple rings on the bottom and sides of the bowl. Chop the remaining pineapple rings. Drain.
4. Cream together the butter and brown sugar until light and fluffy.
5. Add the eggs and beat well.
6. Sift together the flour, baking powder and cinnamon. Add to the egg and sugar mixture and beat well. Add the chopped pineapple. Pour in just enough of the reserved pineapple liquid to give the mixture a not-too-stiff consistency. Pour into the bowl.
7. Cover the bowl with plastic film and cook for 15 minutes or until the cake is done. Remove from the oven, take off the plastic wrap and allow to stand for five minutes before turning upside-down.

Serves 6.

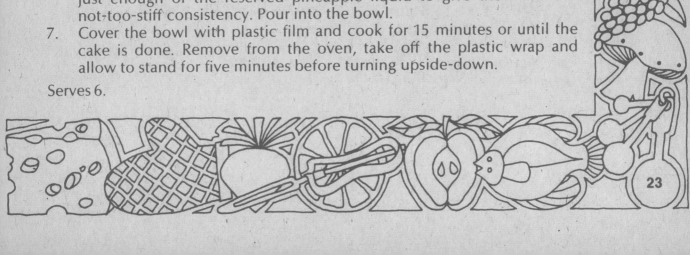

23

Creme Caramel

⅓ cup sugar	½ cup sugar
4 eggs	2½ cups (625 ml) milk
3 egg yolks	1¼ teaspoons vanilla
	nutmeg

1. Put the sugar into a glass or ceramic casserole dish. Place in the microwave oven on the highest setting and cook for about five minutes or until the sugar has melted. Tip the dish to coat the bottom and sides.
2. Combine the egg, egg yolks and sugar.
3. Heat the milk in the oven, then stir into the egg and sugar mixture.
4. Add the vanilla and pour into the coated dish.
5. Cook for 8-10 minutes stirring every two minutes.
6. Cool, then chill for several hours. Turn out of the dish onto a serving platter. Sprinkle with nutmeg and serve.

Serves 6.

Cheesecake Squares

¼ cup (65 g) butter	3 tablespoons sugar
⅔ cup graham cracker crumbs	1 large egg, beaten
1 tablespoon sugar	1 teaspoon vanilla
1 teaspoon cinnamon	grated lemon and orange rind
½ lb (250 g) cream cheese	

1. Melt the butter in a glass mixing bowl in the microwave oven on the highest setting.
2. Stir in the cracker crumbs, sugar and cinnamon.
3. Press the crumb crust into a square glass or ceramic baking dish.
4. Soften the cream cheese and mix with the sugar until smooth.
5. Add the egg and vanilla and mix thoroughly.
6. Spoon the cream cheese mixture into the baking dish.
7. Cook in the microwave oven for two minutes rotating a couple of times during the cooking period.
8. Remove from the oven and sprinkle on the grated orange and lemon rind. Chill before serving.

Egg Dishes

Egg with Ham and Cheese

2 slices ham 4-inch (10-cm)
 square
2 large eggs
salt and black pepper
2 tablespoons grated Swiss
 cheese
sliced stuffed olives

1. Place a slice of the ham into a ramekin or cup fitting it up along the sides. Cover with a paper towel and cook in the microwave oven on the highest setting for one minute.
2. Break the eggs into the ramekins and pierce the yolks. Season to taste with salt and pepper and sprinkle on the grated cheese.
3. Cover and cook for one minute or until the eggs are almost set.
4. Remove from the oven and garnish with stuffed olives. Re-cover and allow to stand for one minute before serving.

Serves 2.

Scrambled Eggs

3 teaspoons butter
3 teaspoons all-purpose flour
½ cup (125 ml) cream
1 tablespoon butter
8 large eggs
½ teaspoon salt
¼ teaspoon black pepper
1 tablespoon minced parsley

1. Melt the three teaspoons butter in a small glass or ceramic bowl, in the microwave oven on the highest setting.
2. Stir in the flour and cook in the oven for 30 seconds.
3. Slowly add the cream, stirring constantly. Return to oven and cook for one minute.
4. Melt the tablespoon of butter in a 10-inch (25-cm) glass pie dish.
5. Lightly beat the eggs with the salt, pepper and parsley. Pour into the pie dish and cook for three to four minutes, or until the eggs are just set. Stir several times during the cooking period.
6. Remove the eggs from the oven and stir in the white sauce. Serve immediately.

Serves 3-4.

Egg with Cheese and Onion

2 teaspoons butter
2 scallions
2 large eggs
salt and pepper
2 tablespoons grated cheese

1. Put one teaspoon of butter into each ramekin or cup. Melt in the microwave oven on the highest setting for ½ minute.
2. Slice one scallion into each ramekin and cook in the oven for two minutes.
3. Break an egg into each ramekin and pierce the yolk. Season to taste with salt and pepper and sprinkle with the cheese. Cover and cook for 45 seconds or until the egg is almost set. Remove from the oven and, leaving covered, allow to stand for one minute before serving.

Serves 2.

Egg with Danish Sausage

4 slices Danish sausage
2 large eggs
1 tablespoon minced chives
salt and pepper
2 tablespoons grated Parmesan
   or Pecorino cheese

1. Chop the Danish sausage into small pieces and place in a ramekin or cup. Cover with a paper towel and cook in the microwave oven on the highest setting for ½ minute.
2. Break an egg into each of the ramekins and pierce the yolk.
3. Sprinkle on the chives, season to taste with salt and pepper and top with the grated cheese.
4. Cover and cook in the oven for 1½ minutes or until the eggs are almost set. Remove from the oven and let stand, covered, for another minute before serving.

Serves 2.

Eggs with Mustard Sauce

8 hard-boiled eggs
3 tablespoons (60 g) butter
3 tablespoons all-purpose flour
1⅔ cups (415 ml) milk
3 teaspoons American mustard
2 tablespoons chopped chives

1. Cut the eggs into halves lengthwise and place on a shallow buttered glass baking dish.
2. Melt the butter in a glass or ceramic dish in the microwave oven.
3. Stir in the flour, then gradually add the milk, stirring constantly.
4. Cook in the oven for three minutes stirring a few times during the cooking period.
5. Stir in the mustard and chives and pour over the eggs.
6. Cook for two minutes and serve immediately.

Serves 4.

Eggs Mornay

3 tablespoons (60 g) butter	8 hard-boiled eggs
3 tablespoons all-purpose flour	1½ teaspoons powdered mustard
1⅔ cups (415 ml) milk	3 tablespoons (60 ml) melted
1 teaspoon salt	butter
½ teaspoon black pepper	salt and pepper
2 cups grated Cheddar cheese	¼ cup (65 ml) cream

1. Melt the butter in an oven-proof dish in the microwave oven on the highest setting.
2. Stir in the flour, then gradually add the milk, stirring constantly. Put into the oven and cook for three minutes stirring a couple of times during the cooking period.
3. Stir in the salt, pepper and 1½ cups cheese. Mix well, then keep warm in a conventional oven until ready to use, or place in the top of a double boiler and put over hot water.
4. Cut the eggs in half lengthwise and remove the yolks.
5. Mash the yolks with the mustard, butter, salt and pepper to taste and the cream. Spoon back into the egg-yolk hole. Arrange the eggs on a glass or ceramic serving dish.
6. Pour the Mornay sauce over the eggs and sprinkle on the remaining cheese. Cook in the oven for two minutes.

Serves 4.

Egg Foo Yung

3 tablespoons (60 g) butter	½ teaspoon grated fresh ginger
6 eggs beaten	½ cup sliced celery
¼ lb (125 g) bean sprouts	½ teaspoon salt
½ cup sliced scallions	¼ teaspoon black pepper
1 clove garlic, minced	soy sauce

1. Melt the butter in a glass or ceramic pie dish in the microwave oven on the highest setting.
2. Mix together the eggs, bean sprouts, scallions, garlic, ginger, celery, salt and pepper.
3. Pour into the dish and cook for about five minutes stirring several times during the cooking period.
4. Serve cut in wedges and sprinkled with soy sauce.

Serves 4.

Fish and Seafoods

Fish with Vegetables

2 tablespoons (40 g) butter
2 lb (1 kg) fish fillets
3 tablespoons (60 g) butter
½ lb (125 g) fresh mushrooms, sliced
1 medium onion, chopped
1 clove garlic, minced
3 tablespoons minced sweet green pepper

3 tablespoons minced sweet red pepper
1 cup chopped tomatoes
¼ cup all-purpose flour
1 teaspoon salt
½ teaspoon black pepper
milk
2 tablespoons lemon juice
minced parsley

1. Melt the butter in a shallow glass or ceramic baking dish in the microwave oven on the highest setting.
2. Arrange the fish in one layer in the dish, cover and cook in the oven for about six minutes or until the fish is cooked through. Turn over half-way through the cooking time. Remove the fish from the dish and put onto a serving platter.
3. Pour any liquid from the dish into a measuring cup. Set aside.
4. Melt the three tablespoons of butter in the dish. Stir in the mushrooms, onion, garlic, green and red pepper and tomatoes. Cover and cook for five minutes, stirring twice during the cooking time.
5. Sprinkle on the flour, salt and pepper and mix well. Cook for two minutes.
6. Add enough milk to the reserved liquid to make up 1½ cups (375 ml). Slowly pour onto the vegetables stirring constantly. Cook for five minutes.
7. Stir the lemon juice into the vegetables then spoon over the fish.
8. Heat the fish and vegetables in the oven if necessary. Serve garnished with chopped parsley.

Serves 6-8.

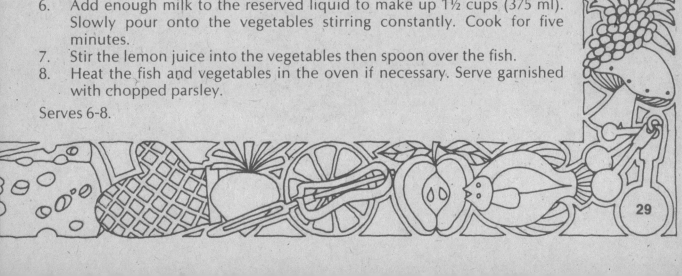

Fish Rolls

¾ lb (375 g) cooked shrimp, minced
1 cup dry bread crumbs
½ teaspoon salt
¼ teaspoon black pepper
¼ teaspoon basil
2 eggs, lightly beaten
⅓ cup (85 ml) lemon juice
2 tablespoons minced parsley
2 teaspoon minced chives

1½ lb (750 g) thin fish fillets
1 cup (250 ml) chicken stock
water
2 tablespoons (40 g) butter
2 tablespoons all-purpose flour
2 tablespoons lemon juice
salt and pepper
lemon wedges
chopped parsley

1. Mix together the shrimp, bread crumbs, salt, pepper, basil, eggs, ⅓ cup lemon juice, parsley and chives.
2. Spread this mixture on the fish fillets, then roll the fish up tucking in the edges. Secure with a wooden toothpick.
3. Put the fish rolls in a shallow glass or ceramic baking dish. Pour the chicken stock over the fish and cover. Cook in the microwave oven on the highest setting for about four minutes or until the fish is cooked through. Turn the fish over once during the cooking time. Remove the fish from the dish.
4. Pour any liquid from the dish into a measuring cup and add enough water to make up ¾ cup (185 ml).
5. Melt the butter in the baking dish and stir in the flour. Cook for ½ minute in the oven.
6. Gradually stir in the ¾ cup of liquid and cook for three minutes or until thickened. Stir a couple of times during the cooking period.
7. Stir the lemon juice into the sauce and season to taste with salt and pepper. Cook for ½ minute in the oven.
8. Pour the sauce over the fish rolls. Re-heat, if necessary. Serve garnished with lemon wedges and chopped parsley.

Serves 4-6.

Fish with Cream Sauce

4-6 fish steaks	½ cup (125 ml) cream
¼ cup (65 g) butter	1 tablespoon dry sherry
1½ tablespoons chopped fresh dill	salt and pepper
	grated lemon rind

1. Rinse the steaks in cold water and pat dry.
2. Melt the butter in a shallow glass or ceramic baking dish with the dill.
3. Add the cream and sherry and mix well. Cook in the microwave oven on the highest setting until heated through.
4. Coat the fish with the cream sauce then arrange in a single layer in the dish.
5. Cook in the oven for six minutes or until the fish is cooked through. Turn the fish over half-way through the cooking time.
6. Season to taste with salt and pepper and sprinkle with grated lemon rind.

Serves 4-6.

Jambalaya

2½ tablespoons (50 g) butter	¼ lb (125 g) ham, diced
2 small onions, chopped	¼ lb (125 g) Italian sausage, diced
2 cloves garlic, minced	1 teaspoon salt
1 sweet green pepper, chopped	½ teaspoon pepper
1 sweet red pepper, chopped	1 bay leaf
1 can (1 lb − 500 g) tomatoes	1 cup rice
2 tablespoons chopped parsley	1 lb (500 g) peeled raw shrimp
1 cup (250 ml) chicken stock	

1. Melt the butter in a glass or ceramic casserole dish in the microwave oven on the highest setting.
2. Add the onions, garlic, green and red pepper and cook for about six minutes, covered, or until vegetables are just tender.
3. Stir in the tomatoes with their liquid, parsley, chicken stock, ham, sausage, salt, pepper, bay leaf and rice. Cover and cook for 15 minutes or until the rice is cooked.
4. Place the shrimp on top of the vegetables and rice, cover and cook for four minutes or until the shrimp are pink. Remove from the oven and allow to stand for five minutes before serving.

Serves 6.

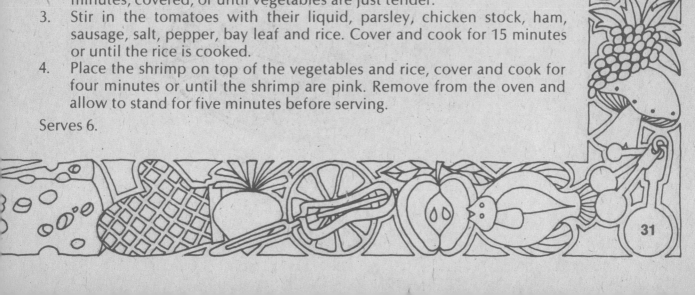

Fish with Mushroom Sauce

¾ cup (185 g) butter
1½ lb (750 g) fish fillets
¼ cup (65 ml) white wine
½ lb (250 g) fresh mushrooms,
  sliced
1 tablespoon chopped parsley

1 small onion, chopped
¼ cup all-purpose flour
½ cup (125 ml) cream
salt
black pepper
½ cup grated Cheddar cheese

1. Melt one-third of the butter in a shallow glass or ceramic baking dish in the microwave oven on the highest setting.
2. Coat the fish with the butter then arrange in a single layer in the dish. Cover and cook in the oven for about five minutes or until the fish is cooked through. Turn the fish over half-way through the cooking time. Remove the fish from the dish and set aside.
3. Pour the liquid from the dish into a cup with the wine. Set aside.
4. Melt another third of the butter in the baking dish and stir in the mushrooms, parsley and onion. Cook for 3-4 minutes stirring several times during the cooking period. Remove the mushroom mixture from the dish and set aside.
5. Melt the rest of the butter in the dish, then stir in the flour. Cook for ½ minute. Stir in the wine mixture and cream and cook for about three minutes or until thickened.
6. Season to taste with salt and pepper.
7. Return the mushrooms to the sauce and mix well.
8. Lay the fish on top of the mushrooms, sprinkle with the cheese and cook until the cheese has melted.

Serves 4-6.

Coquilles St. Jacques

3 tablespoons (60 g) butter
½ lb (250 g) fresh mushrooms, sliced
½ cup minced onions
1 lb (500 g) scallops, diced

½ cup (125 ml) white wine
1½ tablespoons flour
½ teaspoon salt
⅔ cup grated Cheddar cheese
paprika

1. Melt one tablespoon of butter in a shallow glass or ceramic baking dish in the microwave oven on the highest setting.
2. Stir in the mushrooms and onions and cook for three minutes. Stir a few times during the cooking period.
3. Lift the mushrooms out with a slotted spoon and discard the liquid (or reserve for other uses).
4. Put the scallops in the dish with the wine. Cover and cook for two minutes, stirring twice during the cooking time.
5. Remove the scallops with a slotted spoon and pour the liquid into a measuring cup with the wine. Make up to 1½ cups of liquid with water if necessary.
6. Melt the remaining butter in the dish and stir in the flour. Cook for one minute.
7. Slowly add the reserved liquid, stirring constantly. Cook for about three minutes or until thickened. Stir during the cooking.
8. Mix in the salt and cheese and cook for about one minute or until the cheese is melted.
9. Add the mushrooms and scallops and spoon into individual ramekins or shells. Cook in the oven for one minute or until heated through. Sprinkle with paprika and serve.

Serves 4.

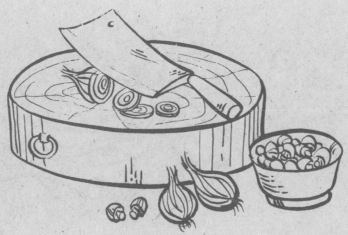

Bream Casserole

1 lb (500 g) bream fillets, cut into cubes
2½ tablespoons (50 g) butter
¼ lb (125 g) fresh mushrooms, sliced
1 small onion, chopped
½ cup sliced celery
2 tablespoons minced parsley
½ cup chopped sweet green pepper
2 tablespoons flour

¾ cup (185 ml) milk
¼ cup (65 ml) dry sherry
1½ teaspoons prepared French mustard
¼ teaspoon Tabasco sauce
¼ teaspoon black pepper
½ cup sliced water chestnuts
¼ cup grated Parmesan cheese
chopped chives

1. Put the fish cubes in a glass or ceramic baking dish. Cover and cook in the microwave oven on the highest setting for about five minutes or until the fish is cooked through. Remove the fish with a slotted spoon and set aside. Discard any liquid.
2. Melt the butter in the dish in the oven, then stir in the mushrooms, onion, celery, parsley and green pepper. Cover and cook for five minutes, stirring several times.
3. Sprinkle on the flour then mix in very well. Cook for one minute.
4. Slowly stir in the milk and cook for about three minutes or until the sauce is thick.
5. Add the sherry, mustard, Tabasco sauce, pepper, water chestnuts, and the fish. Cover and cook for two minutes.
6. Sprinkle on the cheese and cook, uncovered, for another minute.
7. Sprinkle on the chives and serve.

Serves 4.

Scallops in Wine

1½ lb (750 g) scallops
⅔ cup (165 ml) dry white wine
3 tablespoons (60 g) butter
2 tablespoons chopped chives
cayenne pepper

1. Put the scallops into a glass or ceramic baking dish. Pour on the wine, cover and cook in the microwave oven on the highest setting for three minutes, stirring several times during the cooking period.
2. Quarter the scallops and put into individual ramekins or shells. Pour the wine liquid over the scallops.
3. Melt the butter in a glass bowl and spoon over the scallops.
4. Sprinkle the scallops with the chopped chives and top with a dusting of cayenne pepper.
5. Cook for ½ minute to heat through.

Serves 4-6.

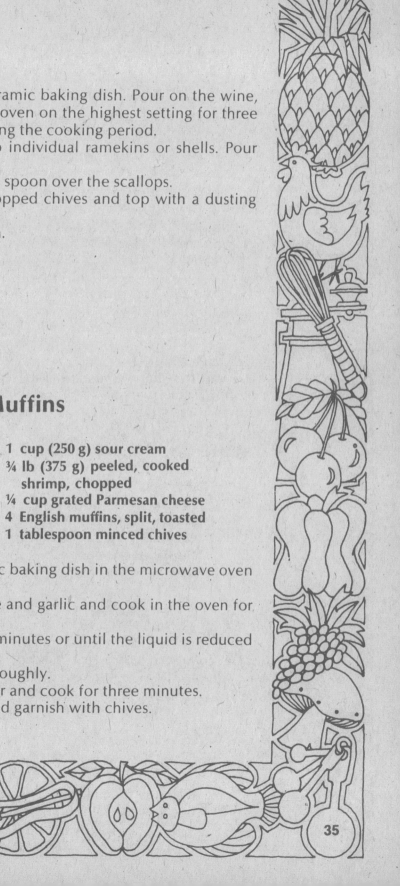

Shrimp and Mushroom Muffins

2½ tablespoons (50 g) butter
½ lb (250 g) fresh mushrooms, sliced
2 tablespoons lemon juice
1 clove garlic, minced
1½ tablespoons dry sherry

1 cup (250 g) sour cream
¾ lb (375 g) peeled, cooked shrimp, chopped
¼ cup grated Parmesan cheese
4 English muffins, split, toasted
1 tablespoon minced chives

1. Melt the butter in a glass or ceramic baking dish in the microwave oven on the highest setting.
2. Stir in the mushrooms, lemon juice and garlic and cook in the oven for about four minutes.
3. Stir in the sherry and cook for five minutes or until the liquid is reduced to half the quantity.
4. Add the sour cream and blend thoroughly.
5. Stir in the shrimp and cheese. Cover and cook for three minutes.
6. Spoon over the buttered muffins and garnish with chives.

Serves 4.

Lobster Tails

2 lobster tails
⅓ cup (85 g) butter, melted
1½ tablespoons lemon juice
⅛ teaspoon Tabasco sauce
black pepper
chopped parsley

1. Cut along the underside of the lobster shells. Peel back the shell and loosen the flesh.
2. Mix together the butter, lemon juice and Tabasco sauce.
3. Put the lobster onto a shallow glass or ceramic baking dish. Pour some of the butter over the lobster, cover and cook in the microwave oven on the highest setting for five minutes. Turn the lobster and pour on more butter several times during the cooking period.
4. Sprinkle on black pepper and serve the lobster garnished with chopped parsley.

Serves 2.

Mussels with Garlic Butter

3 tablespoons (60 g) butter
2 cloves garlic, minced
1 tablespoon chopped parsley
2 teaspoons minced chives
3 teaspoons lemon juice
18 mussels in their shells

1. Mix together the butter, garlic, parsley, chives and lemon juice in a small glass bowl. Put in the microwave oven on the highest setting and cook until the butter is just beginning to bubble.
2. Put the mussels in a glass or ceramic pie dish and cover with plastic wrap. Cook in the oven for about three minutes or until the mussels have opened.
3. Serve with garlic butter.

Serves 2.

Meat Dishes

Chicken Casserole (1)

3 lb (1½ kg) chicken pieces
black pepper
paprika
¼ cup (65 g) butter
2 small onions, chopped
2 cloves garlic, minced
1½ cups sliced celery

1 cup chopped sweet green pepper
2 cups (500 ml) chicken stock
2 egg yolks
¼ cup (65 ml) cream
¼ cup minced parsley
salt
freshly grated pepper

1. Rub the black pepper and paprika on the chicken pieces. Set aside.
2. Melt the butter in a glass or ceramic casserole dish in the microwave oven on the highest setting.
3. Mix in the vegetables, then lay the chicken pieces on top.
4. Pour on the chicken stock, cover and cook in the oven for ½ hour. Remove the chicken from the casserole dish.
5. Blend together the egg yolks and cream. Add a little of the stock from the dish and beat, then stir the egg yolk mixture into the vegetables.
6. Return the chicken to the dish and cook for about two minutes or until heated through.
7. Add the parsley and season to taste with salt and pepper. (This casserole is very "soupy". If desired, thicken the sauce with cornstarch mixed with cold water.)

Serves 4.

Veal with Ham and Cheese

4 pieces veal steak ¼ inch (5 mm)
  thick
flour
salt and pepper
1 egg, lightly beaten

dried bread crumbs
3 tablespoons (60 g) butter
4 slices ham
4 slices Swiss cheese
chopped parsley

1. Pound the veal steaks until thin.
2. Lightly coat with seasoned flour.
3. Dip into the beaten egg, then coat with the bread crumbs.
4. Melt the butter in a glass or ceramic shallow baking dish. Put the veal in the dish and cook in the microwave oven on the highest setting for five minutes. Turn over and cook for another five minutes or until the veal is cooked.
5. Put a slice of ham and a slice of cheese on top of each piece of veal. Put back into the oven and cook until the cheese has melted.
6. Serve immediately garnished with chopped parsley.

Serves 4.

Pork Chops with Mushroom Sauce

½ cup (125 g) butter
½ lb (250 g) fresh mushrooms,
  sliced
2 cloves garlic, minced
1 small onion, chopped
⅔ cup (165 ml) cream
1 teaspoon salt

¼ teaspoon black pepper
2 tablespoons grated Parmesan
  cheese
¼ cup dried bread crumbs
½ teaspoon oregano
4 pork chops
chopped chives

1. Melt half the butter in a glass or ceramic dish.
2. Stir in the mushrooms, garlic and onion and cook in the microwave oven on the highest setting for two minutes. Stir a couple of times during the cooking period.
3. Add the cream, salt and pepper, mix well and cook for another five minutes. Set aside.
4. Mix together the Parmesan cheese, bread crumbs and oregano.
5. Melt the rest of the butter in a shallow glass or ceramic baking dish.
6. Dip the chops with the butter then coat with the bread crumb mixture. Shake off any excess bread crumbs. Place in the dish with the melted butter.
7. Cook in the oven for five minutes. Turn over and cook for another five minutes or until the chops are cooked through. Sprinkle with chopped chives and serve.

Serves 4.

Ground Beef with Spinach and Mushroom

1 lb (500 g) ground beef
1 lb (500 g) fresh spinach
¼ cup (65 g) butter
½ lb (250 g) fresh mushrooms
1 medium onion, chopped
1 tablespoon chopped fresh basil
2 tablespoons chopped parsley

1 clove garlic, minced
1 cup (250 ml) sour cream
1 teaspoon salt
½ teaspoon black pepper
1 cup grated Cheddar cheese
½ cup grated Parmesan cheese

1. Put the beef into a glass or ceramic casserole dish and cook in the microwave oven on the highest setting for five minutes. Stir a few times during the cooking period to break up the beef.
2. Remove the beef from the dish and drain off any fat. Set aside.
3. Cut the central white stem from the spinach and rinse several times in cold water. Chop the spinach coarsely and drain well.
4. Melt the butter in the same dish and stir in the mushrooms, onion, basil, parsley, garlic and spinach. Cover and cook in the oven for three minutes, stirring during the cooking time.
5. Add the meat, sour cream, salt, pepper, half the Cheddar cheese and half the Parmesan cheese. Sprinkle the rest of the cheese on the top.
6. Bake for six minutes in the oven or until the mixture is heated through.

Serves 4.

Lamb's Liver

2 lb (1 kg) lamb's liver
10 black peppercorns
5 whole cloves
1 cup coarsely chopped parsley
2 small onions, quartered

1 cup chopped celery
1 medium carrot, thickly sliced
1 bay leaf
1 teaspoon salt
water

1. Put the liver into a glass or ceramic casserole dish (with a tight-fitting lid) and put the peppercorns, cloves, parsley, onions, celery, carrot, bay leaf and salt over it.
2. Pour on enough water to just cover the ingredients.
3. Cover and cook in the microwave oven on the highest setting for ten minutes.
4. Remove from the oven and allow to stand for five minutes.
5. Turn the liver over and cook in the oven for another ten minutes or until the meat is just cooked.

Serves 6-8.

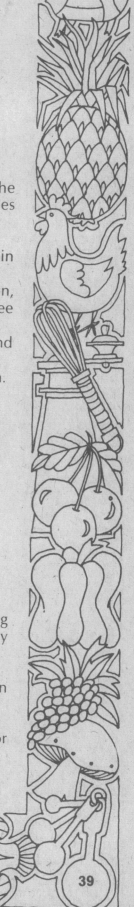

Lasagne

¾ lb (375 g) lasagne noodles
1½ tablespoons olive oil
1 large onion, chopped
2 cloves garlic, minced
2 cups chopped tomatoes
½ cup minced sweet green pepper
1½ lb (750 g) ground beef
½ cup (125 ml) tomato paste

1 cup (250 ml) tomato purée
¼ cup (65 ml) red wine
1 teaspoon salt
½ teaspoon black pepper
½ teaspoon oregano
½ lb (250 g) ricotta cheese
½ lb (250 g) Mozzarella cheese
½ cup grated Parmesan cheese

1. Cook the lasagne noodles in boiling salted water on the top of a conventional stove until tender. Drain and rinse. Cover with warm water and set aside until ready to use.
2. Heat the oil in a glass baking dish in the microwave oven on the highest setting.
3. Stir in the onion and garlic and cook for three minutes.
4. Add the tomatoes and green pepper. Cook for another two minutes, stirring twice during the cooking time.
5. Add the beef and cook for four minutes, stirring frequently during the cooking period to break up the beef. Skim off any fat that accumulates on the top.
6. Mix in the tomato paste, tomato purée, red wine, salt, pepper and oregano. Cook for another two minutes.
7. Put a layer of lasagne noodles on the bottom of a glass baking dish. Spoon on some of the meat sauce. Put on some of the ricotta cheese and slices of the Mozzarella cheese. Continue layering until all the ingredients are used ending with the Parmesan cheese sprinkled on the top.
8. Cook in the oven for about five minutes or until heated through.

Serves 4-6.

Corned Beef with Spinach Sauce

3 lb (1½ kg) corned beef
4 cups (1 liter) hot water
1 bay leaf
10 black peppercorns
1 dried chili pepper
½ teaspoon nutmeg
1 clove garlic, halved
½ teaspoon cumin seeds

½ teaspoon mustard seeds
1 stick cinnamon
½ teaspoon whole coriander
1 onion, quartered
2 lb (1 kg) fresh spinach
3 tablespoons (60 g) butter
3 tablespoons all-purpose flour
2 cups (500 ml) cream

1. Rinse the corned beef under cold water and put into a glass or ceramic casserole dish with the water, bay leaf, peppercorns, chili pepper, nutmeg, garlic, cumin seeds, mustard seeds, cinnamon, coriander and onion.
2. Cover and cook in the microwave oven on the lowest setting for about two hours or until the meat is tender. Turn the meat a few times during the cooking period.
3. While the beef is cooking, cut out the central white stems from the spinach. Wash several times in cold water, then drain and chop the spinach coarsely. Put the spinach in a saucepan and cook, covered, on a conventional stove until the spinach is just tender. Do not add any additional water to the spinach when cooking. Drain the spinach and whirl in an electric blender or press through a sieve.
4. Melt the butter in a saucepan on a conventional stove and remove from the heat. Stir in the flour. Return to the heat and cook for two minutes over a low heat. Season to taste with salt and pepper.
5. Remove from heat and gradually add the cream, stirring constantly. Return to the heat and cook until thick and smooth.
6. Add the spinach and mix well. Keep warm.
7. Remove the corned beef from the oven when cooked and serve with the spinach sauce. (Strain the liquid in which the beef was cooked and reserve as a base for soup or stock.) Serves 8.

Veal Shoulder

3 lb (1½ kg) boned and rolled shoulder of veal
2 cloves garlic, minced
1 teaspoon paprika
½ teaspoon black pepper
1 tablespoon olive oil
3 tablespoons (60 g) butter
1 medium onion, chopped
1 clove garlic, minced
3 tablespoons all-purpose flour
1 cup (250 ml) cream
½ cup (125 ml) water
salt
2 tablespoons chopped parsley

1. Place the veal on a glass or ceramic baking dish.
2. Mix together the garlic, paprika, pepper and oil. Rub onto the veal.
3. Cook in the microwave oven on the highest setting for 15 minutes. Turn the veal over and cook for another 15-20 minutes or until the veal is just tender. Baste with the drippings several times during the cooking period. (The meat will cook for a few minutes after being removed from the oven so allow for that when testing the meat for doneness.) Remove from the baking dish.
4. Melt the butter in the same baking dish stirring well to scrape up the drippings.
5. Add the onion and garlic and cook for three minutes, stirring frequently.
6. Stir in the flour and cook for one minute.
7. Slowly add the cream and water, stirring constantly. Add salt to taste and cook for about five minutes, stirring a few times during the cooking period.
8. Blend in the parsley and serve with the veal.

Serves 6-8.

Knockwurst with Cabbage

3 tablespoons (60 g) butter
2 small onions, chopped
1 clove garlic, minced
1 lb (500 g) cabbage, shredded
1 teaspoon salt
½ teaspoon black pepper
1 lb (500 g) knockwurst, thickly sliced

1. Melt the butter in a glass or ceramic casserole dish in the microwave oven on the highest setting.
2. Stir in the onions and garlic and cook for two minutes.
3. Add the cabbage, salt and pepper and mix well.
4. Lay the knockwurst slices on top of the cabbage. Cover and cook for 12 minutes.

Serves 3-4.

Veal Kidneys with Sour Cream Sauce

1 lb (500 g) veal kidneys
salt and pepper
flour
3 tablespoons (60 g) butter
1 clove garlic, minced
1 cup chopped scallions

1½ tablespoons flour
1 teaspoon mustard
250 g (½ lb) fresh mushrooms, sliced
⅓ cup (85 ml) dry sherry
⅔ cup (165 ml) sour cream

1. Cut the veal kidneys into slices and lightly coat with salt, pepper and flour.
2. Melt the butter in a glass or ceramic shallow baking dish and cook the garlic and shallots for one minute in the microwave oven on the highest setting.
3. Stir in the kidneys and cook, covered, for five minutes. During the cooking time, stir the kidneys once or twice. Remove from the dish.
4. Blend the flour mixed with the mustard into the drippings in the dish. Mix in the mushrooms and sherry and cook for four minutes stirring during the cooking time.
5. Stir in the kidneys and sour cream. Season to taste with salt and pepper, cover and put back into the oven until heated through.

Serves 4.

Frankfurters

4 Continental frankfurters
4 frankfurter buns
butter
mustard
grated Cheddar cheese

1. Put the frankfurters into buttered buns.
2. Spread on a little mustard and sprinkle with grated cheese.
3. Wrap each frankfurter and bun in a piece of paper towel or paper napkin.
4. Place in the microwave oven and cook on the highest setting for 3-4 minutes or until heated through.

Serves 4.

Pork Spareribs

2 small onions, sliced	1 teaspoon grated lemon rind
1 lemon, sliced	1 teaspoon grated fresh ginger
3 lb (1½ kg) pork spareribs	2 cloves garlic, minced
½ cup (125 ml) honey	1 tablespoon cornstarch
½ cup (125 ml) soy sauce	3 tablespoons cold water
⅓ cup (85 ml) lemon juice	chopped chives

1. Place the onions and lemon slices on the bottom of a glass or ceramic baking dish.
2. Put the spareribs on top, cover and cook in the microwave oven on the highest setting for ten minutes.
3. Mix together the honey, soy sauce, lemon juice, lemon rind, ginger and garlic. Pour over the spareribs, cover and cook on the lowest setting for one hour.
4. Remove the spareribs from the dish and skim off any fat.
5. Blend together the cornstarch and water and stir into the sauce in the dish. Mix well and cook for four minutes in the oven until thickened. Mix a few times during the cooking period.
6. Return the spareribs to the dish and spoon the sauce over them. Put back in the oven and cook until heated through. Garnish with chopped chives.

Serves 4.

Glazed Meat Loaf

2 lb (1 kg) ground beef	1 teaspoon salt
2 eggs, lightly beaten	½ teaspoon black pepper
½ cup chopped onions	⅓ cup (85 ml) tomato sauce
½ cup grated carrots	4 tablespoons brown sugar
1 tablespoon German mustard	3 tablespoons German mustard
1 tablespoon tomato paste	

1. Mix together the beef, eggs, onions, carrots, mustard, tomato paste, salt and pepper.
2. Press into a glass loaf dish.
3. Blend together the tomato sauce, brown sugar and mustard and spread on the top of the meat loaf.
4. Cook in the microwave oven on the highest setting for about 25 minutes. Turn the dish around often during the cooking time. Allow to stand for about five minutes before serving.

Serves 6.

Pork with Prune Sauce

2 lb (1 kg) pork, cut into cubes
1 cup (250 ml) prune juice
1 tablespoon lemon juice
1 teaspoon grated lemon rind
2 tablespoons orange juice
1 teaspoon grated orange rind
1 teaspoon grated fresh ginger

¼ teaspoon cinnamon
¼ teaspoon nutmeg
½ teaspoon black pepper
1½ tablespoons cornstarch
3 tablespoons cold water
1½ cups pitted prunes

1. Put the pork cubes into a glass or ceramic casserole dish. Cover and cook in the microwave oven on the highest setting for 15 minutes. Pour off any liquid into a glass bowl or dish, skimming off the fat. Set the pork aside.
3. Add the prune juice, lemon juice and rind, orange juice and rind, ginger, cinnamon, nutmeg and pepper to the liquid in the bowl.
4. Blend the cornstarch with the cold water and add to the prune juice mixture. Cook in the oven for three minutes, stirring frequently during the cooking period.
5. Pour the sauce over the pork. Add the prunes and mix well. Return to the oven and heat through. Serves 6.

Cheeseburgers

1 lb (500 g) ground beef
1 teaspoon salt
½ teaspoon black pepper
1 tablespoon chopped onion
1 tablespoon tomato paste
1 teaspoon Worcestershire sauce
1 egg, lightly beaten
4 hamburger buns

Cheese Topping:
⅔ cup grated Cheddar cheese
2 tablespoons (40 g) soft butter
1½ teaspoons American mustard
1 tablespoon chopped parsley
1 tablespoon minced chives

1. Mix together the beef, salt, pepper, onion, tomato paste, Worcestershire sauce and egg. Form into four hamburgers.
2. Put hamburgers on a glass baking dish and cover with a piece of brown paper. Cook in the microwave oven on the highest setting for about five minutes.
3. Put the hamburgers on the bottom half of the hamburger buns.
4. Mix together the cheese, butter, mustard, parsley and chives. Put on top of the hamburgers.
5. Put on the top of the buns and place on the dish. Cover with a cloth and cook in the oven until the cheese has melted and the hamburgers are heated through.

Serves 4.

Sweet and Sour Beef

½ cup brown sugar
2 tablespoons cornstarch
⅓ cup (85 ml) vinegar
2½ tablespoons soy sauce
1 can (1 lb) pineapple pieces

1 lb (500 g) boneless sirloin steak
1 sweet green pepper, sliced
1 sweet red pepper, sliced
1 large onion, sliced

1. Mix together the sugar, vinegar and soy sauce.
2. Drain the pineapple and reserve the liquid. Measure one cup of the liquid (make up with water, if necessary) and blend with the sugar mixture. Set aside.
3. Cut the steak into thin slices and place on a lightly oiled glass baking dish. Cook in the microwave oven for about four minutes or until it loses its pinkness.
4. Add the peppers and onion and cook for another two minutes.
5. Add the sweet and sour sauce and cook for five minutes, stirring twice during the cooking time.
6. Stir in the pineapple pieces and cook for another two minutes or until heated through.

Serves 4.

Roman Meatballs

1 egg, lightly beaten
2 tablespoons tomato juice
2 teaspoons Worcestershire sauce
½ cup soft bread crumbs
2 tablespoons tomato paste
2 cloves garlic, minced

2 tablespoons minced parsley
3 tablespoons scallions
⅓ cup grated Parmesan cheese
1 lb (500 g) ground beef
½ teaspoon salt
½ teaspoon black pepper
1 teaspoon oregano

1. Mix together the egg, tomato juice, Worcestershire sauce and bread crumbs. Set aside to soak for about ten minutes.
2. Add the tomato paste, garlic, parsley, scallions, grated cheese, beef, salt, pepper and oregano. Blend thoroughly.
3. Form into small meatballs and place in a single layer on a shallow glass baking dish.
4. Cook in the microwave oven on the highest setting for about seven minutes or until cooked. Move the meatballs around on the dish half-way through the cooking time. Serve with spaghetti, spaghetti sauce and Parmesan cheese.

Serves 4.

Cully's Meat Loaf

2 lb (1 kg) ground beef
2 eggs, lightly beaten
1 teaspoon salt
½ teaspoon black pepper
½ cup dry bread crumbs
1 large onion, chopped
1 can (1 lb) condensed tomato
  soup

2 cloves garlic, minced
1 tablespoon Worcestershire
  sauce
2 tablespoons American mustard
2 tablespoons brown sugar
1 teaspoon salt
½ teaspoon black pepper
chopped chives

1. Mix together the ground beef, eggs, salt, pepper and bread crumbs. Set aside.
2. In another bowl combine the onion, tomato soup, garlic, Worcestershire sauce, mustard, brown sugar, salt and pepper.
3. Pour about a quarter of the sauce mixture into the beef mixture. Blend thoroughly.
4. Form the meat mixture into the form of a loaf and place on a shallow glass baking dish.
5. Pour the rest of the sauce over the meat loaf.
6. Bake in the microwave oven on the highest setting for about 25 minutes. Remove from the oven and allow to sit five minutes before serving. Garnish with chopped chives.

Serves 6.

Meatballs

1 egg, lightly beaten
2 tablespoons tomato juice
2 teaspoons Worcestershire
  sauce
½ cup soft bread crumbs
1 tablespoon tomato paste

2 tablespoons minced parsley
3 tablespoons minced scallions
1 lb (500 g) ground beef
1 teaspoon salt
½ teaspoon black pepper

1. Combine the egg, tomato juice, Worcestershire sauce and bread crumbs and allow to stand for about ten minutes.
2. Mix with the tomato paste, parsley, scallions, beef, salt and pepper.
3. Form into small balls and put in a single layer on a shallow glass or ceramic baking dish.
4. Cook in the microwave oven on the highest setting for about seven minutes or until the meatballs are cooked. Move the meatballs around on the dish half-way through the cooking time.

Serves 4.

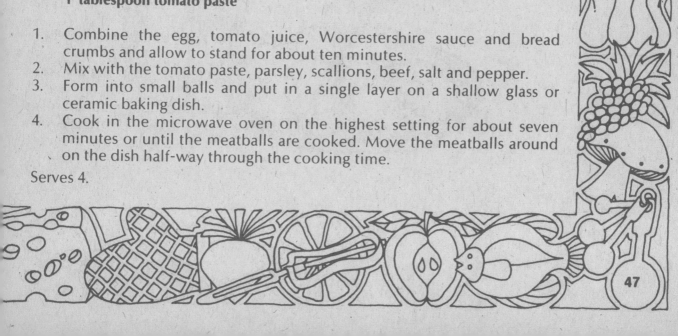

Meatballs with Tomato Sauce

1 egg, lightly beaten
2 tablespoons tomato juice
2 teaspoons Worcestershire
sauce
½ cup soft bread crumbs
1 clove garlic, minced
2 tablespoons minced parsley
2 tablespoons tomato paste
1 cup cooked rice
1 tablespoon minced onions
1 teaspoon salt
½ teaspoon black pepper

Sauce:
1 can (1 lb) tomatoes
⅔ cup chopped sweet green
pepper
2 tablespoons tomato paste
2 cloves garlic, minced
2 tablespoons chopped chives
2 tablespoons chopped parsley
¼ teaspoon Tabasco sauce
½ teaspoon salt
½ teaspoon black pepper

1. Mix together the egg, tomato juice, Worcestershire sauce and bread crumbs. Set aside and allow to soak for about ten minutes.
2. Add the garlic, parsley, tomato paste, rice, onions, salt and pepper. Blend thoroughly.
3. Form into small meatballs and place in a shallow glass baking dish.
4. Chop the canned tomatoes with the liquid and mix with the green pepper, tomato paste, garlic, chives, parsley, Tabasco sauce, salt and pepper.
5. Pour over the meatballs. Cover and cook in the microwave oven on the highest setting for about 15 minutes. Remove from the oven, leave covered and allow to stand for five minutes before serving.

Serves 4.

Meatballs with Curry Sauce

1 egg, lightly beaten
2 tablespoons tomato juice
2 teaspoons Worcestershire
  sauce
½ cup soft bread crumbs
1 tablespoon tomato paste
1 clove garlic, minced
½ teaspoon grated fresh ginger
1 tablespoon minced parsley
2 tablespoon minced onions
1 teaspoon salt
½ teaspoon black pepper
1 lb (500 g) ground beef

Sauce:
1 tablespoon (20 g) butter
1 tablespoon flour
1 teaspoon curry powder (or to
  taste)
1 clove garlic, minced
⅛ teaspoon cayenne pepper
2 tablespoons minced onions
½ cup (125 ml) chicken stock
1 cup (250 ml) cream
salt and pepper

1. Mix together the egg, tomato juice, Worcestershire sauce and bread crumbs. Set aside and allow to soak for about ten minutes.
2. Add the tomato paste, garlic, ginger, parsley, onions, salt, pepper and beef. Blend thoroughly and form into small meatballs.
3. Place in a single layer on a shallow glass baking dish and cook in the microwave oven on the highest setting for about seven minutes or until cooked.
4. Remove the meatballs from the dish and add the butter. Melt in the oven.
5. Stir in the flour, curry powder, garlic, cayenne pepper and onions. Cook in the oven for ½ minute.
6. Gradually add the chicken stock and cream. Cook in the oven for about six minutes or until thickened. Stir several times during the cooking period. Season to taste with salt and pepper.
7. Return the meatballs to the dish and roll around in the sauce to ensure that each meatball is covered. Cover and cook in the oven for two minutes or until hot.

Serves 4.

Baked Ham

½ cup (125 ml) orange
  marmalade
1 teaspoon grated orange rind
2 tablespoons French mustard
¼ teaspoon nutmeg
¼ teaspoon ground cloves
1 can cooked ham

1. Mix together the marmalade, orange rind, mustard, nutmeg and cloves.
2. Put the ham in a glass or ceramic baking dish.
3. Spread the marmalade mixture on top and cook in the microwave oven on the highest setting for about five minutes or until heated through. Spoon the sauce over the ham a couple of times during the cooking period.

Serves 6.

Fruity Lamb Stew

2 lb (1 kg) stewing lamb, cut into
  cubes
1½ teaspoons salt
½ teaspoon black pepper
1 teaspoon grated fresh ginger
2 cloves garlic, minced
½ teaspoon cinnamon
2 cups (500 g) tomato juice

2 cups diced carrots
1 large onion, chopped
¼ lb (125 g) dried apricots
¼lb (125 g) dried apples
¼ lb (125 g) raisins
1 cup chopped pitted prunes
1½ tablespoons cornstarch
¼ cup (65 ml) cold water

1. Mix the lamb cubes with the salt, pepper, ginger, garlic, cinnamon and tomato juice in a glass or ceramic casserole dish. Cover and cook in the microwave oven on the lowest setting for 20 minutes.
2. Add the carrots, onion, apricots, apples, raisins and prunes. Mix well, cover and cook on the highest setting for 15 minutes or until the meat and fruit are cooked.
3. Blend the cornstarch with the water and stir into the stew. Return to the oven and cook until thickened (about two minutes).

Serves 6-8.

Chicken with Bananas

4 chicken legs with thighs
½ cup (125 ml) tomato sauce
1 tablespoon brown sugar
1 tablespoon lemon juice
1 tablespoon vegetable oil

½ cup minced onions
1 clove garlic, minced
1 tablespoon minced parsley
1 teaspoon Worcestershire sauce
2 cups sliced bananas

1. Place the chicken pieces on a shallow glass or ceramic baking dish.
2. Mix together the tomato sauce, brown sugar, lemon juice, vegetable oil, onions, garlic, parsley and Worcestershire sauce.
3. Pour over the chicken, then turn the chicken over several times to ensure that it is well-coated.
4. Cook in the microwave oven on the highest setting for ten minutes. Turn the dish several times during the cooking period.
5. Add the bananas and spoon the sauce over them. Cook for another three minutes, or until the chicken is just cooked. Remove from the oven and allow to stand for five minutes before serving.

Serves 4.

Chicken Casserole (2)

3 lb (1½ kg) chicken pieces
2 tablespoons (40 g) butter
¼ lb (125 g) fresh mushrooms, sliced
1 clove garlic, minced
1 medium onion, chopped

½ cup cracked wheat
2 teaspoons chopped fresh rosemary
salt and pepper
1 cup (250 ml) chicken stock
1 cup grated Edam cheese
paprika

1. Put the chicken pieces in a shallow glass or ceramic baking dish. Cook in the microwave oven on the highest setting for 20 minutes or until the chicken is tender. Rotate the dish a quarter of a turn every five minutes. Remove the chicken from the oven and set aside. Pour off any juices from the dish and reserve.
2. Melt the butter in a glass or ceramic casserole dish.
3. Stir in the mushrooms, garlic and onion and cook for two minutes stirring a couple of times.
4. Stir in the wheat, rosemary, salt and pepper to taste, chicken stock and the reserved juices. Cover and cook for about seven minutes or until the liquid is absorbed.
5. Add the chicken pieces, cover and cook for two minutes.
6. Sprinkle on the cheese and paprika and cook until the cheese melts.

Serves 4.

Hot Chicken Sandwiches

1½ cups chopped cooked chicken
¼ cup (65 ml) mayonnaise
¼ cup sliced scallions
1 tablespoon minced parsley
1 teaspoon German mustard

2 teaspoons prepared horseradish
salt and pepper
4 toasted hamburger buns, buttered

1. Mix together the chicken, mayonnaise, scallions, parsley, mustard, horseradish and salt and pepper to taste.
2. Divide the mixture into quarters and spread on each of the hamburger buns.
3. Wrap the filled hamburger buns in paper towels.
4. Place in the microwave oven on the highest setting for 30 seconds. Allow to stand for one minute before serving.

Serves 4.

Chicken with Sausages

½ lb (250 g) Italian sausage, sliced
1 cup frozen peas
1 cup (250 ml) chicken stock
4 chicken legs with thighs

salt and pepper
paprika
3 teaspoons cornstarch
1½ tablespoons cold water
chopped parsley

1. Put the sausage and peas on the bottom of a shallow glass or ceramic baking dish.
2. Pour the chicken stock oven them, then lay the chicken on top. Season to taste with salt and pepper and sprinkle generously with paprika.
3. Cover and cook in the microwave oven on the highest setting for about 20 minutes, turning the dish a quarter of a turn every five minutes.
4. When the chicken is cooked, put onto a serving platter.
5. Blend the cornstarch with the cold water, then stir into the sausage and pea mixture. Cook in the oven for two minutes or until thick, stirring frequently.
6. Pour over the chicken and garnish with chopped parsley.

Serves 4.

Chicken with Asparagus

2 cups cooked brown rice
½ cup pine nuts
1 lb (500 g) sliced asparagus
1 cup (250 ml) chicken stock
⅓ cup (85 ml) dry white wine
1 medium onion, chopped

1 teaspoon salt
½ teaspoon black pepper
1 teaspoon grated lemon rind
1 tablespoon lemon juice
3 lb (1½ kg) chicken pieces
paprika

1. Mix together the rice, pine nuts, asparagus, chicken stock, wine, onion, salt, pepper, lemon rind and lemon juice. Spread over the bottom of a shallow glass or ceramic baking dish.
2. Put the chicken pieces on the rice-asparagus mixture and sprinkle with paprika.
3. Cover and cook in the microwave oven at the highest setting for about 20 minutes. Rotate the dish a quarter of a turn every five minutes. When the chicken is cooked, allow to stand for five minutes before serving.

Serves 4.

Chicken with Cheese and Ham

1½ lb (750 g) raw white chicken
   meat
slices Swiss cheese
slices ham
3 tablespoons (60 g) butter
salt and pepper

paprika
¼ lb (125 g) fresh mushrooms,
   sliced
¼ cup (65 ml) dry sherry
chopped chives

1. Pound each piece of chicken until thin.
2. Place a slice of Swiss cheese and a slice of ham on each piece of chicken. Fold over and secure with a wooden toothpick.
3. Melt the butter in a shallow glass or ceramic baking dish.
4. Coat the chicken with the melted butter, then sprinkle generously with salt, pepper and paprika. Remove from dish.
5. Stir the mushrooms into the butter and cook in the microwave oven on the highest setting for one minute stirring twice.
6. Put the chicken on top of the mushrooms and cook for five minutes.
7. Place the chicken on a serving dish and stir the sherry into the mushrooms. Spoon the mushrooms over the chicken and garnish with chopped chives.

Serves 4.

Parmesan Chicken

½ cup grated Parmesan cheese
½ cup dried bread crumbs
½ teaspoon oregano
½ teaspoon black pepper

½ cup (125 g) butter
8 chicken legs
chopped parsley

1. Mix together the Parmesan cheese, bread crumbs, oregano and pepper.
2. Melt the butter in a glass or ceramic shallow baking dish. Brush the melted butter on the chicken legs.
3. Thoroughly coat the chicken legs in the Parmesan cheese mixture.
4. Place in the baking dish and cook for five minutes. Turn the chicken legs around in the dish and cook for another five minutes or until chicken is just cooked. Allow to stand for five minutes after removing from the oven.
5. Sprinkle with chopped parsley and serve.

Serves 4.

Chicken with Cheese Sauce

1½ lb (750 g) raw white chicken meat
½ teaspoon paprika
¼ teaspoon black pepper
2 teaspoons cornstarch

2½ tablespoons dry sherry
½ cup (125 ml) cream
½ cup grated Cheddar cheese
2 tablespoons grated Parmesan cheese

1. Put the chicken meat into a glass or ceramic shallow baking dish.
2. Mix together the paprika, black pepper and cornflour. Add the sherry and cream and blend thoroughly.
3. Pour the cream mixture over the chicken, cover and cook for three minutes in the microwave oven at the highest setting, stirring a few times during the cooking period.
4. Mix together the Cheddar and Parmesan cheeses and sprinkle on the chicken. Cook for about two minutes or until the cheese is melted and the chicken is cooked.

Serves 4.

Chicken Paprika

⅔ cup all-purpose flour
3 teaspoons paprika
1 teaspoon salt
½ teaspoon black pepper

½ cup (125 g) butter
4 chicken breasts
chopped chives

1. Mix together the flour, paprika, salt and pepper.
2. Melt the butter in a glass or ceramic shallow baking dish in the microwave oven on the highest setting.
3. Dip the chicken breasts in the melted butter.
4. Thoroughly coat the chicken with the flour-paprika mixture.
5. Place in the oven meat side down and cook for five minutes. Turn over chicken and rotate the dish. Cook for another seven minutes or until the chicken is just cooked. Allow to stand for five minutes before serving. Garnish with chopped chives.

Serves 4.

Japanese Chicken

1 tablespoon sesame seeds
3 lb (1½ kg) chicken pieces
½ cup (125 ml) soy sauce
3 tablespoons brown sugar
¼ cup (65 ml) dry sherry
1 tablespoon cornstarch

¼ cup (65 ml) chicken stock
½ teaspoon grated fresh ginger
2 cloves garlic, minced
1 cup sliced scallions
3 tablespoons (60 g) butter, melted

1. Toast the sesame seeds in the microwave oven on the highest setting in a glass or ceramic baking dish for two minutes or until golden brown. Remove from dish and set aside.
2. Put the chicken pieces in the baking dish, meat side down, and cook for about six minutes. Remove from oven.
3. Mix together the soy sauce, brown sugar, sherry, cornstarch, chicken stock, ginger and garlic in a glass mixing bowl. Cook in the oven for 1½ minutes, stirring frequently.
4. Spoon the soy sauce mixture over the chicken pieces and cook for another six minutes.
5. Turn the chicken over, spoon over some more sauce and cook for a further six minutes or until the chicken is cooked.
6. Pour the melted butter over the chicken pieces, sprinkle with scallions and toasted sesame seeds. Put in the oven until heated through. If there is any sauce remaining, heat and serve separately with the chicken.

Serves 4.

Chicken with Plum Sauce

1 can (1 lb — 500 g approx) plums
2 tablespoons (40 g) butter
1 medium onion, chopped
1 clove garlic, minced
3 tablespoons brown sugar
2 tablespoons tomato paste

½ teaspoon chili powder
2 tablespoons soy sauce
1 tablespoon lemon juice
½ teaspoon grated fresh ginger
1 tablespoon minced chives
1 chicken (3 lb — 1½ kg), whole

1. Drain the plums and remove the stones. Put the plums into an electric blender and whirl until smooth or press through a sieve. Set aside.
2. Melt the butter in a glass or ceramic baking dish in the microwave oven on the highest setting.
3. Stir in the onion and garlic and cook for two minutes in the oven.
4. Mix together the brown sugar, tomato paste, chili powder, soy sauce, lemon juice, ginger and chives. Stir in the puréed plums and blend thoroughly. Add to the onion and garlic and cook for five minutes stirring twice during the cooking time. Pour the sauce into another dish.
5. Put the chicken into the cleaned baking dish and cook for five minutes.
6. Spread the sauce over the chicken and cook for seven minutes.
7. Turn the chicken over and cook for another six minutes, spreading with more sauce and basting a couple of times during the cooking time.
8. Put the chicken onto a serving dish. Pour the drippings from the dish into a glass bowl with the sauce. Heat in the oven.
9. Carve the chicken and serve with the plum sauce.

Serves 4.

Lamb with Peaches

2 lb (1 kg) boneless lamb, cut into cubes
1 teaspoon salt
½ teaspoon black pepper
1 teaspoon cinnamon
1 teaspoon cloves
1 teaspoon grated lemon rind
½ teaspoon nutmeg
2 tablespoons lemon juice
2½ tablespoons brown sugar

2 small onions, chopped
3 teaspoons cornstarch
2 tablespoons cold water
2 tablespoons (40 g) butter
6 fresh peaches, peeled and sliced
⅔ cup (165 g) sour cream
1 tablespoon lemon juice
chopped parsley

1. Put the lamb in a shallow glass or ceramic baking dish.
2. Blend together the salt, pepper, cinnamon, cloves, lemon rind, nutmeg, lemon juice, brown sugar, and onions. Spoon over the top of the lamb.
3. Cover the dish and cook in the microwave oven on the lowest setting for ½ hour or until the lamb is tender. Stir twice during the cooking time.
4. Blend the cornstarch with the cold water in a small glass bowl. Spoon off some of the liquid from the lamb and mix into the cornstarch mixture. Cook in the oven on the highest setting for three minutes stirring during the cooking time. Pour over the lamb when thickened.
5. Cover and cook in the oven until the mixture is heated through.
6. Melt the butter in a glass baking dish and stir in the peaches. Cook in the oven until the peaches are heated through. Mix in with the lamb.
7. Mix the sour cream with the lemon juice.
8. Serve the lamb and peaches with the sour cream mixture spooned on top of each serving and sprinkled with chopped parsley.

Serves 4-6.

Lamburgers

1 lb (500 g) ground lamb
1 tablespoon minced onion
3 tablespoons dried bread crumbs
1 large egg, beaten
2 tablespoons chopped raisins
1 clove garlic, minced
¼ teaspoon ginger

½ teaspoon curry powder
¼ teaspoon cinnamon
¼ teaspoon black pepper
1 teaspoon salt
½ cup (125 g) plain yogurt
2 tablespoons fruit chutney
4 hamburger buns

1. Combine the lamb, onion, bread crumbs, eggs, raisins, garlic, ginger, curry powder, cinnamon, pepper and salt.
2. Form into four patties and place on a glass shallow baking dish. Cover with a piece of paper and cook in the microwave oven on the highest setting for about six minutes or until cooked to your liking. Half-way through the cooking, turn the lamburgers over.
3. Mix together the yogurt and chutney.
4. Place the lamburgers on the buns, spread on the yogurt mixture and wrap in paper. Cook in the oven until heated through.

Serves 4.

Marinated Lamb Chops

8 lamb chops
½ cup (125 ml) red wine
1 teaspoon Worcestershire sauce
2 tablespoons olive oil
½ teaspoon grated fresh ginger
2 cloves garlic, minced

1 small onion, minced
1 teaspoon salt
½ teaspoon black pepper
2 tablespoons chopped parsley
½ teaspoon nutmeg
¼ teaspoon cinnamon

1. Put the chops in a shallow glass or ceramic baking dish.
2. Combine the wine, Worcestershire sauce, oil, ginger, garlic, onion, salt, pepper, parsley, nutmeg and cinnamon.
3. Pour over the chops. Turn the chops over several times to ensure that they are well-coated with the marinade. Cover and allow to marinate for at least five hours in the refrigerator.
4. Pour off the marinade and cook the chops in the microwave oven at the highest setting for six minutes. Turn over half-way through the cooking time. Allow to stand for five minutes before serving.

Serves 4.

Apricot Duck

4 lb (2 kg) duck
½ cup (125 g) apricot jam
¼ cup (65 ml) chicken stock
3 teaspoons soy sauce
½ teaspoon grated fresh ginger

1 tablespoon powdered mustard
2 teaspoons grated orange rind
2 teaspoons cornstarch
1½ tablespoons cold water
2 teaspoons minced chives

1. Put the duck in a shallow glass or ceramic baking dish, breast side down. Prick the skin with a fork. Cook in the microwave oven on the highest setting for ten minutes rotating the dish a couple of times during the cooking period.
2. Mix together the apricot jam, chicken stock, soy sauce, ginger, mustard and orange rind.
3. Drain the liquid from the baking dish. Spread the apricot jam mixture on the duck and cook for another ten minutes.
4. Turn the duck breast side up, spread on the jam mixture and cook for another ten minutes.
5. Pour the drippings into a small bowl. Skim off the fat.
6. Blend together the cornstarch and cold water. Mix into the bowl with the drippings and any left-over jam mixture. Cook in the oven for one minute, stirring a couple of times.
7. Carve the duck and pour the sauce over the servings. Garnish with chopped chives.

Serves 4.

Buttered Fish

1½ lb (750 g) fish fillets
¼ cup (65 g) butter
1 tablespoon minced fresh dill
1 teaspoon grated lemon rind

salt and pepper
1 tablespoon chopped parsley
slices lemon

1. Rinse the fish fillets in cold water. Pat dry.
2. Melt the butter in a shallow glass or ceramic baking dish. Add the dill, lemon rind, salt and pepper.
3. Coat the fillets with the butter then place in a single layer in the dish.
4. Cover and cook in the microwave oven on the highest setting for five minutes, turning the fish over half-way through the cooking time.
5. Remove from the oven and allow to stand for about three minutes before serving.
6. Serve garnished with chopped parsley and lemon slices.

Serves 4-6.

Beef and Noodles

1 lb (500 g) ground beef
3 teaspoons vegetable oil
2 small onions, chopped
2 cloves garlic, minced
1 sweet red pepper, chopped
2 medium tomatoes, chopped
2 tablespoons chopped parsley

½ cup (125 ml) beef stock
½ cup (125 ml) cream
¼ cup tomato paste
2 cups cooked noodles
1 teaspoon salt
½ teaspoon black pepper

1. Put the meat into a large glass or ceramic casserole dish and cook in the microwave oven on the highest setting for two minutes, stirring a few times during the cooking period to keep the meat broken up. Remove the meat from the dish and discard any fat. Set aside.
2. Heat the vegetable oil in the casserole dish, then add the onions, garlic and red pepper. Cook for two minutes.
3. Add the tomatoes and parsley and cook for another minute.
4. Stir in the cooked beef, beef stock, cream, tomato paste, noodles, salt and pepper. Cover and cook for eight minutes, rotating the dish a quarter of a turn after five minutes.

Serves 4.

Beef Torte

1 lb (500 g) frozen bread dough
1 lb (500 g) ground beef
1 cup chopped ham
1 medium onion, chopped
1 clove garlic, minced
1 teaspoon salt

½ teaspoon black pepper
1 tablespoon tomato paste
3 tomatoes, sliced
½ cup grated Parmesan cheese
½ cup grated Cheddar cheese
¼ cup (65 ml) cream

1. Thaw the bread and divide into quarters. Roll out to fit a glass or ceramic casserole dish.
2. Oil the dish and place one piece of the dough on the bottom.
3. Mix together the ground beef, ham, onion, garlic, salt, pepper and tomato paste. Spread a layer of this mixture over the dough. Continue layering until all the ingredients are used up, ending with a layer of dough.
4. Lay the slices of tomato on the dough.
5. Mix together the Parmesan cheese and Cheddar cheese and sprinkle on top of the tomatoes. Pour on the cream.
6. Cover and bake in the microwave oven on the highest setting for about eight minutes, turning the dish a quarter of a turn every two minutes. Allow to stand for five minutes before serving.

Serves 6.

Beef Stew

1 tablespoon (20 g) butter	3 medium carrots, sliced
2 tablespoons olive oil	½ lb (250 g) potatoes, peeled and cut up
2 small onions, sliced	3 tablespoons tomato paste
2 cloves garlic, minced	1 cup (250 ml) beef stock
1 sweet green pepper, chopped	1 teaspoon Worcestershire sauce
2 lb (1 kg) chuck, cut into cubes	1 bay leaf
flour	water
salt and pepper	salt and pepper

1. Heat the butter and olive oil in a large glass or ceramic casserole dish.
2. Stir in the onions and garlic and cook in the microwave oven on the highest setting for ½ minute.
3. Add the green pepper, mix well and cook for another minute.
4. Coat the cubes of chuck steak with seasoned flour. Add to the casserole dish and cook for five minutes.
5. Stir in the carrots, potatoes, tomato paste, beef stock, Worcestershire sauce and bay leaf. Add just enough water to cover. Stir well, cover and cook in the oven on a low setting for 45-50 minutes or until the beef is tender. Season to taste with salt and pepper.
6. This stew is best if left overnight and re-heated in the oven the next day.

Serves 6.

Chili Con Carne

1 lb (500 g) ground beef	¼ teaspoon cayenne pepper
2 tablespoons olive oil	1 teaspoon salt
1 onion, minced	3 tablespoons tomato paste
2 cloves garlic, minced	1 can (1 lb) tomatoes
1 teaspoon chili powder or to taste	¼ teaspoon Tabasco sauce
	2 cups red kidney beans, drained

1. Put the beef in a glass or ceramic casserole dish. Cook in the microwave oven on the highest setting for two minutes stirring a few times to keep the meat broken up. Set aside.
2. Pour the olive oil into a small glass bowl and heat in the oven for ½ minute.
3. Add the onion and garlic and cook for one minute.
4. Stir in the chili powder and cayenne pepper and cook for 45 seconds.
5. Stir the onion mixture into the beef with the salt, tomato paste, tomatoes and Tabasco sauce. Mix thoroughly and cook for five minutes, stirring several times during the cooking period.
6. Add the kidney beans and cook for a further two minutes. (Chili Con Carne is delicious served with fluffy white rice.)

Serves 4-6.

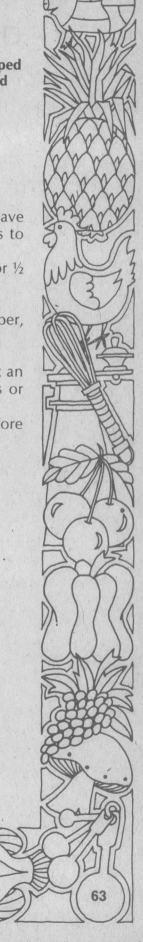

Egg and Beef Bake

½ lb (250 g) ground beef
¼ cup (65 ml) vegetable oil
2 onions, chopped
2 cloves garlic, minced
1 small eggplant, peeled and cut into cubes
1 cup (250 ml) tomato purée
¼ cup (65 g) tomato paste

1 small sweet green pepper, chopped
1 small sweet red pepper, chopped
1 teaspoon salt
½ teaspoon black pepper
2 teaspoons Worcestershire
1½ cups cooked white rice
6 eggs
2 tablespoons minced parsley

1. Put the beef into a glass or ceramic bowl and cook in the microwave oven on the highest setting for two minutes, stirring several times to keep the meat broken up. Skim off any fat and set aside.
2. Pour the oil into a glass or ceramic pie dish and heat in the oven for ½ minute.
3. Stir in the onions and garlic and cook for one minute.
4. Add the eggplant, tomato purée, tomato paste, green and red pepper, salt, pepper and Worcestershire sauce. Cook for one minute.
5. Add the beef and cook for another three minutes, stirring twice.
6. Stir in the rice, then make six indentations in the mixture and break an egg in each indentation. Cover and cook for about eight minutes or until the eggs are set.
7. Remove from the oven and allow to stand for three minutes before serving.
8. Serve garnished with minced parsley.

Serves 6.

Herbed Lamb

5 lb (2½ kg) leg of lamb
⅔ cup dried bread crumbs
½ cup minced parsley
1 tablespoon minced fresh basil
2 teaspoons minced fresh rosemary

¼ cup (65 g) butter
3 cloves garlic, minced
1 tablespoon minced chives
salt
freshly grated black pepper

1. Bone the lamb and flatten as much as possible. Put the lamb, fat side down, on a roasting rack for microwave ovens or place on an inverted saucer in a glass or ceramic baking dish.
2. Blend together the bread crumbs, parsley, basil and rosemary. Spread on the lamb.
3. Put the butter, garlic and chives in a small glass bowl and heat in the microwave oven for 45 seconds on the highest setting. Drip the mixture over the bread crumb mixture.
4. Cook the lamb in the oven on the highest setting for ten minutes. Rotate the dish and cook for another seven minutes.
5. Remove from the oven and season to taste with salt and pepper. Allow to stand for five minutes before serving.

Serves 6-8.

Lamb Stew

1½ lb (750 g) stewing lamb
flour
salt and pepper
¼ cup (65 ml) vegetable oil
2 tablespoons tomato paste
½ cup (125 ml) white wine
2½ cups (625 ml) chicken stock
1 clove garlic, minced

½ lb (250 g) potatoes, peeled and quartered
½ lb (250 g) carrots, sliced
2 small onions, quartered
½ lb (250 g) green beans
2 tablespoons chopped parsley
salt
freshly grated black pepper

1. Cut the lamb into cubes and coat with flour seasoned with salt and pepper.
2. Heat the oil in a glass or ceramic casserole dish in the microwave oven on the highest setting.
3. Stir in the lamb, cover and cook for ten minutes, stirring several times during the cooking period.
4. Mix the tomato paste with the wine, then blend with the chicken stock. Pour over the meat and mix well.
5. Add the garlic, potatoes, carrots, onions, beans and parsley. Cover and cook for about ½ hour or until the lamb is tender. Season to taste with salt and pepper. Allow to stand for about five minutes before serving.

Serves 4.

Stewed Lamb Shanks

¼ cup (65 ml) vegetable oil
6 lamb shanks
3 tablespoons all-purpose flour
2 cups (500 ml) chicken stock
2 tablespoons tomato paste

2 small onions, sliced
1 lb (500 g) tomatoes, quartered
2 cloves garlic, minced
½ lb (250 g) carrots, sliced
salt and pepper

1. Heat the oil in a large skillet on a conventional stove. Add the lamb shanks and brown on all sides. Put the shanks in a glass or ceramic casserole dish.
2. Stir the flour into the oil in the skillet stirring up any scrapings from the bottom of the pan. Add the chicken stock and tomato paste, stirring until smooth.
3. Add the onions, tomatoes, garlic and carrots. Mix well, then pour over the lamb shanks. Cover and cook in the microwave oven for about 45 minutes or until the lamb shanks are tender. Season to taste with salt and pepper.

Serves 6.

Orange Chicken

1 chicken (3 lb — 1½ kg)
1½ cups (375 ml) orange juice
2 tablespoons lemon juice
2 tablespoons grated orange rind
2 teaspoons grated lemon rind
¼ cup brown sugar
½ teaspoon grated fresh ginger

2 tablespoons (40 ml) melted
   butter
1 tablespoon cornstarch
¼ cup (65 ml) water
2 teaspoons soy sauce
orange slices
slivered almonds

1. Put the chicken in a glass or ceramic baking dish breast side down.
2. Mix together the orange juice, lemon juice, orange rind, lemon rind, sugar, ginger and melted butter. Pour over the chicken.
3. Cook the chicken in the microwave oven on the highest setting for 15 minutes basting frequently with the sauce. Turn the chicken over and cook for another ten minutes, or until the chicken is tender. Put the chicken on a warm serving dish.
4. Blend the cornstarch with the water and soy sauce. Stir into the dripping in the baking dish. Put in the oven and cook for two minutes or until thick, stirring a few times.
5. Pour the sauce over the chicken and garnish with orange slices and slivered almonds.

Serves 4.

Orange Pork

3 cups diced cooked pork
2 tablespoons vegetable oil
2 small onions, chopped
1 cup raw white rice
½ teaspoon salt
¼ teaspoon black pepper
1 teaspoon paprika
½ teaspoon nutmeg

⅓ cup pine nuts
⅓ cup raisins
2 cups (500 ml) chicken stock
¾ cup (185 ml) orange juice
1 teaspoon grated orange rind
1 tablespoon (20 g) butter
orange slices
slivered almonds

1. Make sure there is no fat on the pork. Set aside.
2. Heat the vegetable oil in a glass or ceramic casserole dish in the microwave oven on the highest setting.
3. Stir in the onions and cook for one minute.
4. Add the rice, mix well and cook for another minute, stirring twice during the cooking time.
5. Add the pork, salt, pepper, paprika, nutmeg, pine nuts, raisins, chicken stock, orange juice, grated orange rind and butter. Mix thoroughly, then cover and cook for eight minutes. Turn the dish a quarter of a turn and cook for another four minutes. Remove from the oven and allow to stand for five minutes.
6. Put the orange slices and slivered almonds on a plate and heat in the microwave oven. Arrange on top of the pork and serve.

Serves 4-6.

Soups

Tomato Madrilene with Avocado

1½ tablespoons gelatin	¼ teaspoon Tabasco sauce
2 cups (500 ml) tomato juice	¼ teaspoon black pepper
1 tablespoon chopped chives	2 cups diced avocados
2 cups (500 ml) beef stock	sour cream
1 tablespoon Worcestershire sauce	minced chives

1. Mix the gelatin with ½ cup of the tomato juice and set aside for ten minutes.
2. Pour into a large glass or ceramic dish and stir in the rest of the tomato juice. Cover and place in the microwave oven. Cook on the highest setting for three minutes.
3. Add the beef stock, Worcestershire sauce, Tabasco sauce and pepper. Put in the refrigerator and chill until thickened.
4. Pour the soup into individual soup bowls and stir in the diced avocado. Chill for several hours before serving.
5. Put a spoonful of sour cream on top of each bowl and garnish with minced chives.

Serves 4.

Broccoli Soup

2 lb (1 kg) fresh broccoli
4 cups (1 liter) chicken stock
¼ cup (65 g) butter
1 medium onion, chopped
salt and pepper
1 cup (250 ml) cream

1. Wash and drain the broccoli. Chop coarsely.
2. Put the broccoli into a large glass or ceramic dish with half the chicken stock. Cover and cook in the microwave oven on the highest setting for three minutes or until the broccoli is tender.
3. Stir in the butter, onion and salt and pepper to taste.
4. Whirl in an electric blender until smooth.
5. Return to the dish and stir in the rest of the chicken stock and the cream.

Serves 4-6.

Asparagus Soup

2 tablespoons (40 g) butter
1 medium onion, chopped
1 clove garlic, minced
1 cup diced potatoes
2 cups (500 ml) water

1 lb (500 g) fresh asparagus
1 teaspoon salt
½ teaspoon black pepper
2 cups (500 ml) cream
¼ cup minced parsley

1. Melt the butter in a glass or ceramic casserole dish or soup tureen in the microwave oven on the highest setting.
2. Stir in the onion and garlic and cook for two minutes.
3. Add the potatoes and one cup of water. Cover and cook for five minutes or until the potatoes are tender. Stir once or twice during the cooking period.
4. Break off the coarse white ends of the asparagus. Wash the spears several times in cold water, then cut into bite-size pieces. Add to the potatoes with the rest of the water. Cook for about five minutes or until the asparagus are tender.
5. Add the salt, pepper and cream. Mix well. Cover and cook for two minutes or until heated through. Do not allow to boil.
6. Stir in the parsley and serve immediately.

Serves 4-6.

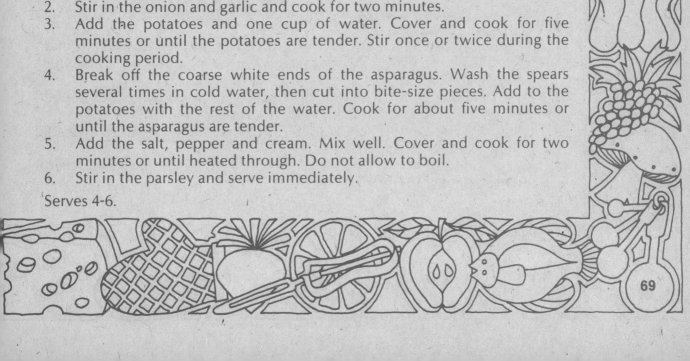

Beet Soup

6 cups peeled, diced beets
4 cups (1 liter) chicken stock
2 cups (500 ml) milk or
   buttermilk
1 teaspoon fresh dill

salt and pepper
2 tablespoons minced chives
1 tablespoon lemon juice
   sour cream

1. Put the beets into a glass or ceramic dish with one cup of the chicken stock. Cook in the microwave oven on the highest setting for 20 minutes or until the beets are tender.
2. Pour into an electric blender with another cup of the chicken stock and whirl until smooth. Return to the dish and stir in the rest of the stock, the milk or buttermilk, dill, salt and pepper to taste, chives and lemon juice. Chill for several hours before serving.
3. Serve with a spoonful of sour cream.

Serves 6-8.

Fish and Vegetable Soup

2 tablespoons olive oil
2 small onions, chopped
2 cloves garlic, minced
½ cup chopped celery
½ cup chopped sweet green
   pepper
2 tablespoons chopped parsley
1 tablespoon chopped chives

1 tablespoon chopped fresh basil
¼ teaspoon cayenne pepper
1½ cups (375 ml) tomato purée
¼ cup (65 g) tomato paste
4 cups (1 liter) chicken stock
1 lb (500 g) white fish fillets
salt and pepper

1. Heat the oil in a glass or ceramic casserole dish in the microwave oven on the highest setting.
2. Stir in the onions, garlic, celery and pepper. Cover and cook in the oven for eight minutes.
3. Add the parsley, chives, basil, cayenne pepper, tomato purée, tomato paste and chicken stock. Mix well. Cover and cook for five minutes.
4. Add the fish fillets and season to taste with salt and pepper and cook for another ten minutes. Stir a few times during the cooking period.

Serves 6.

Orange and Carrot Soup

2 tablespoons olive oil
2 small onions, chopped
1 lb (500 g) carrots, sliced
4 cups (1 liter) chicken stock
1 teaspoon brown sugar

1 teaspoon fresh dill
2 cups (500 ml) fresh orange
   juice
salt
chopped chives

1. Heat the oil in a glass or ceramic casserole dish or soup tureen in the microwave oven on the highest setting.
2. Stir in the onions. Cover and cook in the oven for two minutes.
3. Add the carrots, one cup of the stock, the sugar and dill. Cover and cook for ten minutes or until the carrots are tender. Stir a couple of times during the cooking time.
4. Pour the soup into an electric blender and whirl until smooth. Pour back into the dish.
5. Stir in the remaining chicken stock and the orange juice. Season to taste with the salt.
6. Cover and chill for several hours before serving.
7. Serve with chopped chives sprinkled on top.

Serves 6.

Vegetable Soup

2 tablespoons (40 g) butter
1 cup chopped scallions
1 medium onion, chopped
2 cloves garlic, minced
1½ cups chopped celery
½ cup chopped parsley
1 cup chopped sweet red pepper

1 cup diced carrots
1 medium turnip, diced
1 cup diced potatoes
4 cups (1 liter) chicken stock
¼ teaspoon marjoram
salt and pepper

1. Melt the butter in a large glass or ceramic dish in the microwave oven on the highest setting.
2. Stir in the scallions, onion, garlic, celery, parsley, pepper and carrots. Cover and cook for ten minutes.
3. Add the turnip, potatoes and one cup of the chicken stock. Cover and cook for about 12 minutes or until the potatoes are tender.
4. Remove about one cup of the soup and whirl in an electric blender or press through a sieve. Return to the soup.
5. Add the rest of the chicken stock. Stir in the marjoram and season to taste with salt and pepper.
6. Cover and cook for another five minutes.

Serves 6.

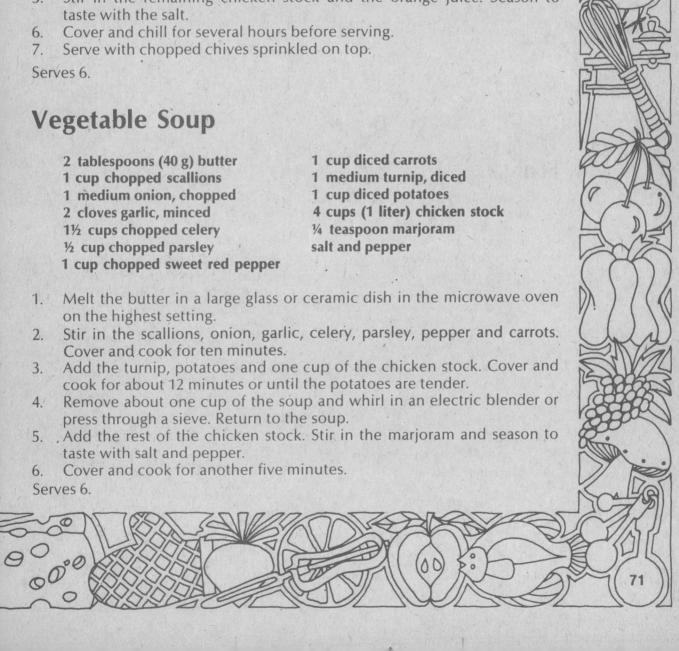

Beef and Cabbage Soup

1 lb (500 g) ground beef
1 small onion, chopped
1 clove garlic, minced
½ lb (250 g) tomatoes, chopped
3 cups (750 ml) beef stock
2 tablespoons tomato paste

1 can (1 lb) kidney beans
1 teaspoon salt
½ teaspoon black pepper
3 cups finely sliced cabbage
croutons
chopped parsley

1. Put the beef into a glass or ceramic casserole dish and cook in the microwave oven on the highest setting for five minutes. Stir often to keep the meat broken up.
2. Add the onion and garlic and cook, covered, for five minutes.
3. Add the tomatoes, beef stock, tomato paste and kidney beans with their liquid. Cover and cook for seven minutes.
4. Stir in the salt, pepper and cabbage. Cover and cook for four minutes. Stir a few times during the cooking.
5. Serve garnished with croutons and chopped parsley.

Serves 6.

Cold Mushroom Soup

¼ cup (65 g) butter
½ lb (250 g) fresh mushrooms, chopped
2 small onions, minced
½ cup chopped parsley

1 tablespoon flour
3 cups (750 g) chicken stock
1½ cups (375 g) sour cream
chopped chives

1. Melt the butter in a glass or ceramic dish in the microwave oven at the highest setting.
2. Stir in the mushrooms, onions and parsley and cook for five minutes. Stir a couple of times during the cooking.
3. Sprinkle on the flour, then stir in half the chicken stock. Cook for one minute.
4. Pour the mushrooms and liquid into an electric blender and whirl until smooth.
5. Add the rest of the chicken stock and whirl again.
6. If there is enough room in the blender, add the sour cream, too. Otherwise pour the soup into a dish and stir in the sour cream.
7. Cover and chill for several hours before serving. Serve garnished with chopped chives.

Serves 4-6.

Sausage Soup

½ lb (250 g) Italian sausage
½ lb (250 g) fresh spinach
2 tablespoons (40 g) butter
2 small onions, minced
1 clove garlic, minced

2 tablespoons flour
1¼ cups (300 ml) cream
4 cups (1 liter) beef stock
salt and pepper

1. Cut the sausage into thin slices. Set aside.
2. Wash the spinach very well several times in cold water. Remove the central white stem and chop the spinach coarsely. Drain the spinach well. Set aside.
3. Melt the butter in a ceramic or glass casserole dish in the microwave oven.
4. Stir in the onions and garlic, cover and cook in the oven for four minutes. Stir a couple of times during the four minutes.
5. Sprinkle on the flour, then stir in the cream. Cook for one minute.
6. Stir in the beef stock, sausage and spinach. Season to taste with salt and pepper. Cover and cook for five minutes. Stir a couple of times during the cooking time.

Serves 4-6.

Tomato Soup

2½ lb (1¼ kg) fresh tomatoes
1 medium onion, minced
⅔ cup minced celery
1 clove garlic, minced
2 tablespoons minced parsley
4 cups (1 liter) chicken stock

2 tablespoons tomato paste
1 tablespoon minced fresh basil
1 teaspoon dried oregano
½ teaspoon black pepper
1 teaspoon salt
1 cup (250 g) sour cream

1. Peel and dice the tomatoes.
2. Put into a glass or ceramic casserole dish with the onion, celery, garlic, parsley, chicken stock, tomato paste, basil, oregano, pepper and salt.
3. Cook in the microwave oven at the highest setting for 15 minutes.
4. Press through a fine sieve to remove the seeds.
5. Stir in the sour cream. Serve cold or warm.

Serves 6.

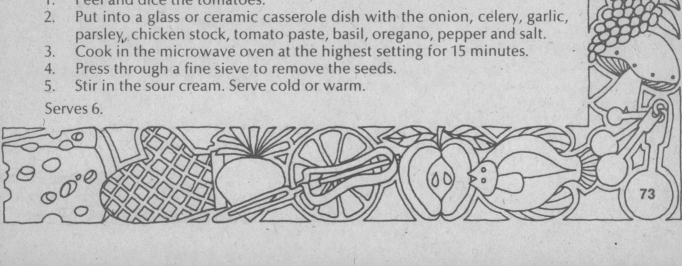

Kidney Bean Soup

½ lb (250 g) bacon, chopped
2 cloves garlic, minced
2 small onions, minced
1 lb (500 g) canned tomatoes
2 lb (1 kg) canned red kidney
  beans

½ teaspoon Tabasco sauce
½ teaspoon thyme
¼ cup (65 ml) vinegar
2 cups (500 ml) beef stock
salt and pepper
chopped chives

1. Put the bacon in a large glass or ceramic casserole dish or soup tureen. Put into the microwave oven at the highest setting and cook, covered for four minutes or until the bacon is crisp. Stir a couple of times during the cooking. Remove the bacon with a slotted spoon and drain on absorbent paper.
2. Stir the garlic and onion into the bacon fat and cook, covered, for four minutes.
3. Add the tomatoes and kidney beans with their liquid.
4. Stir in the Tabasco sauce, thyme, vinegar and beef stock. Cover and cook for about ten minutes.
5. Take out about two cups of the soup and mash or purée. Return to the dish and stir well.
6. Season to taste with salt and pepper. Heat through, if necessary. Serve with chopped chives.

Serves 6.

Cream of Spinach Soup

2 lb (1 kg) fresh spinach
1 small onion, minced
½ cup chopped celery
1½ cups diced potatoes
1 teaspoon salt

½ teaspoon black pepper
¼ teaspoon nutmeg
6 cups (1½ liters) chicken stock
1½ cups (375 ml) cream
½ cup diced ham

1. Wash the spinach several times in cold water. Drain then remove the white central stems. Discard the stems and chop the spinach leaves.
2. Put the spinach into a glass or ceramic casserole dish with the onion, celery, potatoes, salt, pepper, nutmeg and stock. Cover and cook on the highest setting for ten minutes.
3. Pour into an electric blender and whirl until smooth.
4. Pour back into the casserole dish and stir in the cream and ham. Cook for another five minutes in the oven. Serve hot.

Serves 6-8.

Onion Soup

⅓ cup (85 g) butter
6 medium onions, sliced
1 clove garlic, minced
1 tablespoon flour
6 cups (1½ liters) beef stock
⅓ cup (85 ml) dry sherry

salt
black pepper
slices French bread, toasted and
    buttered
1 cup grated Swiss cheese

1. Melt the butter in a glass or ceramic casserole dish in the microwave oven on the highest setting.
2. Add the onions and garlic and mix well. Cook in the oven, covered, for 15 minutes, stirring frequently during the cooking time.
3. Sprinkle with the flour.
4. Add the beef stock, sherry, salt and pepper to taste. Cover and cook for eight minutes. Stir a couple of times during the cooking time.
5. Put a piece of toasted and buttered French bread in the bottom of each soup bowl. Pour the soup over it and sprinkle with the grated cheese. Place the bowls in the microwave oven for about one minute or until the cheese melts.

Serves 6-8.

Frankfurter and Corn Sauce

1 lb (500 g) frankfurters
1½ tablespoons olive oil
2 small onions, chopped
1 medium potato, diced
1 sweet red pepper, chopped
1 sweet green pepper, chopped
1½ cups corn kernels

3 cups (750 ml) chicken stock
1 cup (250 ml) cream
½ cup sliced stuffed olives
¼ teaspoon cumin
salt
freshly ground white pepper

1. Cut the frankfurters into thin slices and put into a glass or ceramic casserole dish with the olive oil. Cover and cook in the microwave oven on the highest setting for two minutes. Remove the frankfurters from the dish and set aside.
2. Add the onions to the oil in the dish, cover and cook for two minutes.
3. Add the potato, peppers, corn and chicken stock, cover and cook for seven minutes. Stir a couple of times.
4. Add the frankfurters, cream, olives, cumin and salt and pepper to taste. Cook for about three minutes or until heated through.

Serves 4.

75

Lamb Hot Pot

2 lb (1 kg) boneless lamb
6 cups (1½ liters) beef stock
1½ teaspoons salt
½ teaspoon black pepper
1 clove garlic, minced
2 medium onions, sliced
2½ tablespoons (50 g) butter
3 teaspoons flour
⅔ cup chopped celery

1 cup diced carrots
½ cup chopped scallions
1 cup corn kernels
1½ cups cauliflower flowerets
1 cup fresh peas
⅔ cup diced potatoes
⅔ cup diced yams
½ cup (125 ml) dry sherry
chopped chives

1. Cut the lamb into bite-size pieces discarding any fat.
2. Put the lamb into a glass or ceramic casserole dish with the beef stock, salt, pepper, garlic and onions. Cover and cook in the microwave oven for ½ hour. Remove from the oven.
3. Melt the butter in a small glass bowl in the oven. Remove from the oven and stir in the flour until smooth. Add a little of the stock from the soup and mix well, then pour the flour and butter mixture into the soup.
4. Add the celery, carrots, scallions, corn, cauliflower, peas, potatoes and yams. Cook for 15 minutes.
5. Stir in the sherry and serve warm sprinkled with chopped chives.

Serves 6-8.

Shrimp and Tomato Soup

1½ lb (750 g) fresh tomatoes
2 small onions, chopped
4 cups (1 liter) chicken stock
1 tablespoon tomato paste
¼ cup (65 ml) dry sherry

1½ cups (375 ml) cream
1 teaspoon salt
½ teaspoon black pepper
½ teaspoon oregano
1 lb (500 g) chopped cooked shrimp

1. Peel and slice the tomatoes.
2. Put the tomatoes into a glass or ceramic casserole dish with the onions, chicken stock and tomato paste. Mix well and cook in the microwave oven at the highest setting for 25 minutes.
3. Pour the soup into an electric blender and whirl until smooth. Pour through a strainer to remove the seeds.
4. Add the sherry, cream, salt, pepper, oregano and prawns. Cook in the oven for ten minutes. Serve warm.

Serves 6.

Mushroom Soup with Shrimp

¾ lb (375 g) button mushrooms,
    halved
1 medium onion, chopped
1½ tablespoons lemon juice
½ teaspoon grated lemon rind
2 tablespoons dry sherry
2 tablespoons (40 g) butter

2 tablespoons flour
3 cups (750 ml) milk
1½ cups (375 ml) cream
½ lb (250 g) peeled, cooked and
    diced shrimp
salt and pepper
minced parsley

1. Mix the mushrooms with the onion, lemon juice, lemon rind and sherry in a small glass bowl. Cover and cook in the microwave oven at the highest setting for two minutes. Remove from the oven and set aside.
2. Melt the butter in the oven then stir in the flour until smooth. Cook for 15 seconds.
3. Stir in the milk and cream gradually. When well-blended, cook for four minutes in the oven. Stir a couple of times during the four minutes.
4. Add the mushroom mixture and the shrimp. Season to taste with salt and pepper and cook for one minute. Serve either hot or cold. Garnish with parsley.

Serves 6.

Cream of Asparagus Soup

1½ lb (750 g) fresh asparagus
½ cup chopped scallions
½ cup diced carrots
1 cup chopped celery
2 tablespoons chopped parsley
2 cups diced potatoes

1 teaspoon salt
½ teaspoon white pepper
4 cups (1 liter) chicken stock
1 cup (250 ml) cream
sour cream
chopped parsley

1. Wash the asparagus several times in cold water. Snap off the white ends of the asparagus. Cut the rest into ½-inch (1-cm) lengths.
2. Put the asparagus into a glass or ceramic casserole dish with the scallions, carrots, celery, parsley, potatoes, salt, pepper and chicken stock. Cook in the microwave oven on the highest setting for ten minutes or until the asparagus are tender.
3. Pour the soup into an electric blender and whirl until smooth.
4. Pour back into the casserole dish and stir in the cream. Cook for another five minutes in the oven.
5. Serve hot with a spoonful of sour cream on the top and sprinkled with chopped parsley.

Serves 6.

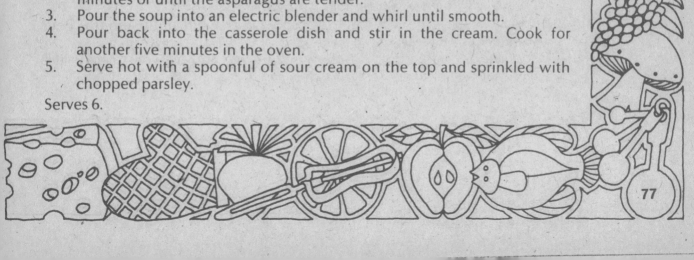

Chicken and Peanut Soup

1½ lb (750 g) chicken pieces	½ cup peanut butter
1 small onion, sliced	¼ cup (65 ml) dry sherry
1 teaspoon salt	1½ cups (375 ml) milk
½ teaspoon black pepper	½ cup (125 g) sour cream
2 tablespoons olive oil	chopped parsley
1 clove garlic, minced	chopped peanuts
1 small onion, chopped	

1. Put the chicken pieces in a glass or ceramic casserole dish with the sliced onion, salt and pepper. Cover and cook in the microwave oven on the highest setting for ½ hour. Remove the chicken pieces and cool until easy to handle. Remove the skin and bones from the chicken and cut the meat into bite-size pieces. Set aside. Strain the stock.
2. Heat the olive oil in a glass or ceramic dish. Add the chopped onion and garlic and cook for two minutes.
3. Pour the onion, garlic and oil into an electric blender with the peanut butter. Whirl until smooth.
4. Skim any fat from the stock and stir in the peanut butter mixture.
5. Pour into a large saucepan and simmer for ten minutes on the top of the stove.
6. Add the milk, sherry and chicken and mix well. Simmer for another few minutes. Remove from heat and cool. Chill for several hours.
7. Before serving, stir in the sour cream and heat through. Serve garnished with parsley and chopped peanuts.

Serves 6.

Chicken and Vegetable Soup

2 lb (1 kg) chicken pieces
6 cups (1½ liters) water
1 medium onion, chopped
1 clove garlic, minced
1 cup diced carrots
½ cup chopped celery

1 cup fresh peas
¼ cup chopped parsley
2 teaspoons chopped fresh
   thyme
salt
white pepper, freshly ground

1. Put the chicken pieces into a glass or ceramic casserole dish with the water, onion, garlic, carrots and celery. Cover and cook in the microwave oven at the highest setting for ½ hour.
2. Remove the chicken from the broth and cool until you can handle it. Remove the skin and bones from the chicken and chop the meat. Discard the skin and bones.
3. When the chicken stock has cooled slightly, skim the fat from the top.
4. Stir the peas, parsley and thyme into the stock and cook for two minutes.
5. Add the chicken and salt and pepper to taste. Cook for another two minutes and serve hot.

Serves 6.

Hungarian Goulash Soup

¼ cup (65 ml) olive oil
4 medium onions, thinly sliced
2 cloves garlic, minced
1 tablespoon paprika
½ lb (250 g) ground beef
¼ lb (125 g) ground veal
6 cups (1½ liters) beef stock

salt
black pepper
2 cups diced potatoes
1 cup chopped tomatoes
2 tablespoons tomato paste
chopped parsley

1. Heat the olive oil in a ceramic or glass casserole dish in the microwave oven on the highest setting.
2. Stir in the onions and garlic and cook for two minutes.
3. Add the paprika, mix well and cook for ½ minute.
4. Mix together the beef and veal and stir into the onion mixture. Cook for two minutes in the oven, stirring half-way through the cooking time to break up the meat.
5. Add the stock and salt and pepper to taste. Cook for five minutes.
6. Add the potatoes, tomatoes and tomato paste, mixing very well. Cook for seven minutes.
7. Serve hot garnished with chopped parsley.

Serves 6-8.

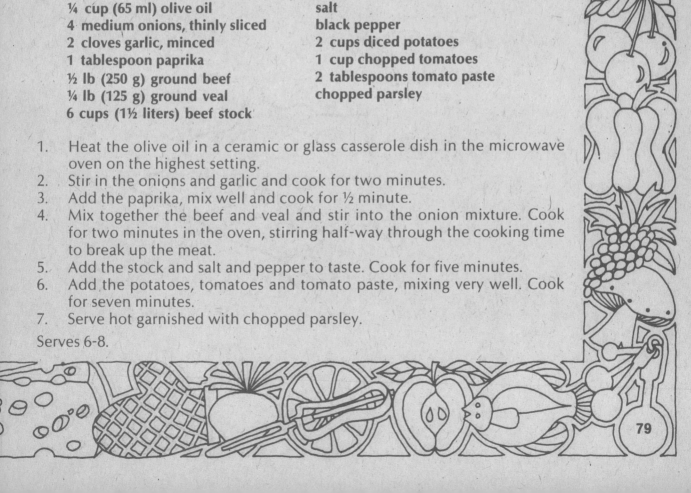

Cream of Corn Soup

4 cups (1 liter) chicken stock
1 large onion, minced
1 cup diced potato
1 cup chopped celery
1 clove garlic, minced
2 tablespoon minced parsley

1½ cups corn kernels, fresh or canned
1½ cups (375 ml) cream
2 egg yolks, lightly beaten
1 teaspoon salt
½ teaspoon white pepper

1. Pour the chicken stock into a glass or ceramic casserole dish and add the onion, potato, celery, garlic and parsley. Cover and cook in the microwave oven on the highest setting for five minutes or until the potatoes are soft.
2. Purée in an electric blender or press through a sieve.
3. Stir in the corn and one cup of the cream. Cook in the oven for two minutes.
4. Blend the egg yolks with the rest of the cream and add to the soup. Cook for ½ minute.
5. Add the salt and pepper and serve warm.

Serves 6.

Corn and Crab Soup

¼ cup (65 g) butter
⅓ cup all-purpose flour
6 cups (1½ liters) milk
½ lb (250 g) cooked crab meat
2 cups corn kernels

1 teaspoon salt
¼ teaspoon white pepper
½ cup (125 ml) cream
minced chives

1. Melt the butter in a glass or ceramic casserole dish in the microwave oven on the highest setting.
2. Add the flour and stir until smooth.
3. Gradually add the milk, stirring constantly, until well-blended.
4. Cook for about five minutes stirring a couple of times to keep the sauce smooth.
5. Cut the crab into small bits and add to the sauce with the corn, salt and pepper. Cover and cook for five minutes.
6. Stir in the cream and serve hot garnished with minced chives.

Serves 4.

Vichyssoise

2 lb (1 kg) potatoes
1½ lb (750 g) leeks
6 cups (1½ liters) chicken stock
1½ cups (375 ml) cream

1¼ teaspoons salt
½ teaspoon freshly ground black pepper
chopped chives

1. Peel and dice the potatoes. Put into a glass or ceramic casserole dish.
2. Slice the white part and some of the green part of the leeks. Rinse under cold water several times. Drain well. Put into the casserole dish with the potatoes.
3. Pour the chicken stock over the potatoes and leeks, cover and cook on the highest setting in the microwave oven for about ten minutes or until the potatoes are soft.
4. Pour into an electric blender and whirl until smooth or press through a sieve.
5. Stir in the cream, salt and pepper.
6. Serve garnished with chopped chives.

Serves 6-8.

Watercress Soup

½ lb (250 g) watercress
¼ cup (65 g) butter
2 small onions, minced
1 clove garlic, minced
⅔ cup minced celery
1 lb (500 g) potatoes, peeled and diced

4 cups (1 liter) chicken stock
1½ tablespoons lemon juice
1 teaspoon salt
½ teaspoon black pepper
¼ teaspoon nutmeg
⅔ cup (165 ml) cream

1. Wash the watercress well in cold water. Drain and chop.
2. Put the butter in a ceramic or glass casserole dish and melt in the microwave oven on the highest setting.
3. Stir in the onions, garlic and celery and cook for two minutes.
4. Add the potatoes, chicken stock, lemon juice, salt, pepper and nutmeg. Cover and cook for 15 minutes.
5. Pour into an electric blender and whirl until smooth.
6. Stir in the cream and chill for several hours or overnight before serving.

Serves 4-6.

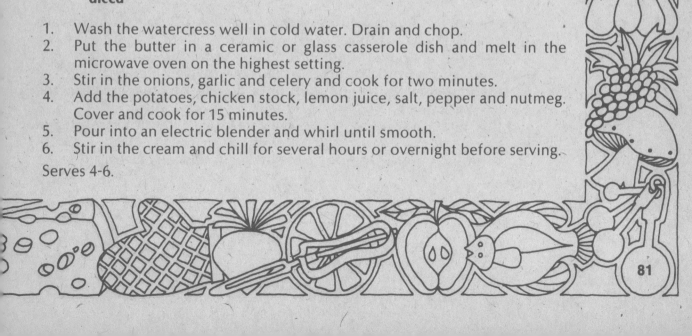

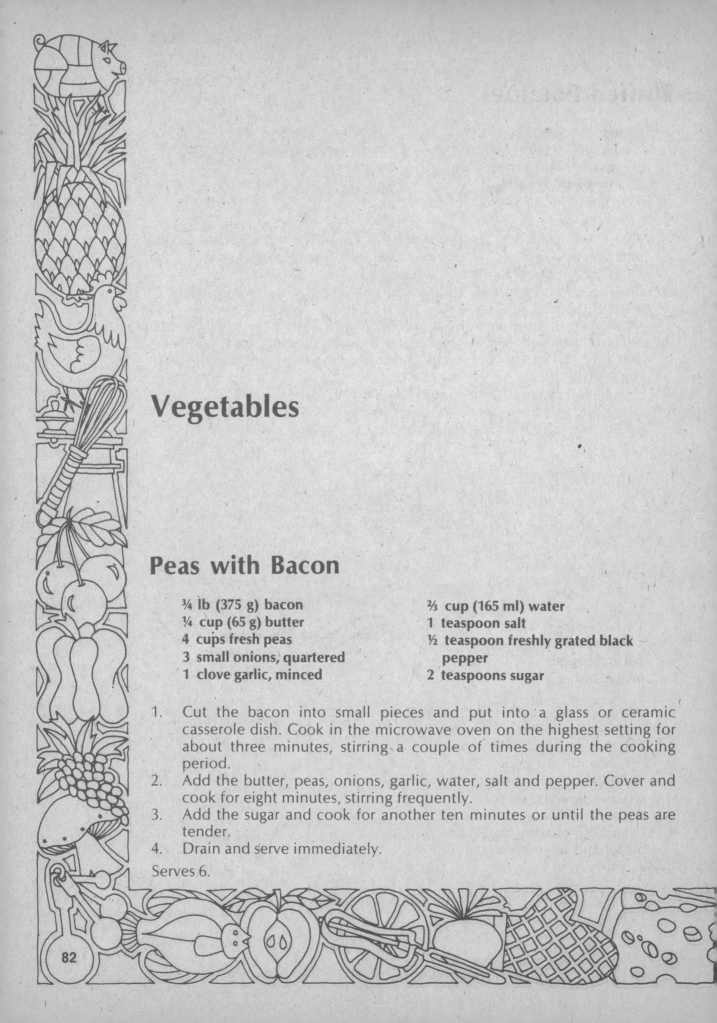

Vegetables

Peas with Bacon

¾ lb (375 g) bacon	⅔ cup (165 ml) water
¼ cup (65 g) butter	1 teaspoon salt
4 cups fresh peas	½ teaspoon freshly grated black
3 small onions, quartered	pepper
1 clove garlic, minced	2 teaspoons sugar

1. Cut the bacon into small pieces and put into a glass or ceramic casserole dish. Cook in the microwave oven on the highest setting for about three minutes, stirring a couple of times during the cooking period.
2. Add the butter, peas, onions, garlic, water, salt and pepper. Cover and cook for eight minutes, stirring frequently.
3. Add the sugar and cook for another ten minutes or until the peas are tender.
4. Drain and serve immediately.

Serves 6.

Stuffed Potatoes

4 large potatoes
2 tablespoons (40 g) butter
2 egg yolks, lightly beaten
2 tablespoons cream
1 teaspoon salt

½ teaspoon white pepper
1½ cups grated Cheddar cheese
⅓ cup minced scallions, white and
   green parts
paprika

1. Pierce the potatoes several times with a skewer and place in the microwave oven on paper towels. Cook on the highest setting for about 12 minutes or until soft when pierced.
2. Cut the potatoes in half and scoop out the potato taking care not to break the skin.
3. Mash the potatoes with the butter, egg yolks, cream, salt and pepper. Beat until smooth. (An electric beater is especially good for this.)
4. Add one cup of the cheese and the scallions. Fill the potato skins with the mixture.
5. Sprinkle on the rest of the grated cheese and a little paprika.
6. Return to the oven and cook for five minutes, rotating the potatoes one-quarter of a turn half-way through the cooking time.

Serves 4-8.

Asparagus

1½ lb (750 g) fresh asparagus
1½ tablespoons water
1 tablespoon lemon juice
salt and pepper
melted butter

1. Wash the asparagus spears several times in cold water. Drain well and snap off the tough ends.
2. Lay the asparagus on a shallow glass or ceramic baking dish with the tips towards the center.
3. Sprinkle on the water and lemon juice. Cover and cook in the microwave oven on the highest setting for about eight minutes or until the asparagus are just tender.
4. Drain and season to taste with salt and pepper. Pour on the melted butter and serve immediately.

Serves 4-6.

Bean Sprouts

⅓ cup (85 g) butter
1 clove garlic, minced
1 tablespoon minced chives
1 lb (500 g) bean sprouts
salt and pepper

1. Melt the butter in a shallow glass or ceramic baking dish in the microwave oven on the highest setting.
2. Stir in the garlic and chives and cook until the butter is bubbling.
3. Add the bean sprouts and mix well. Cover and cook for 5-7 minutes or until they begin to wilt.
4. Season to taste with salt and pepper and serve immediately.

Serves 4-6.

Broccoli Casserole

1 lb (500 g) fresh broccoli
½ cup (125 ml) water
⅓ cup (85 g) butter
2 small onions, chopped
1 clove garlic, minced
2 tablespoons chopped parsley
3 tablespoons flour
¾ cup (185 ml) milk
1½ cups grated Cheddar cheese
3 eggs, lightly beaten
½ teaspoon salt
¼ teaspoon black pepper
¼ teaspoon nutmeg
¼ cup sesame seeds

1. Wash the broccoli well. Drain and coarsely chop.
2. Put the chopped broccoli into a glass or ceramic casserole dish with the water. Cover and cook in the microwave oven on the highest setting for seven minutes or until the broccoli is tender. Drain and set aside.
3. Melt the butter in the same casserole dish. Mix in the onions, garlic and parsley and cook for three minutes.
4. Stir in the flour and cook for one minute, stirring a couple of times.
5. Slowly add the milk, stirring constantly. Cook for another minute, stirring twice.
6. Stir in the cheese until it melts.
7. Add the drained broccoli, eggs, salt, pepper and nutmeg. Cook for seven minutes, stirring at least twice during the cooking period.
8. Sprinkle on the sesame seeds and cook for about four minutes or until the mixture is set. Allow to stand for about five minutes after removing from the oven before serving.

Serves 6.

Brussels Sprouts

¼ cup (65 ml) water
2 teaspoons lemon juice
1 teaspoon grated lemon rind
1 lb (500 g) Brussels sprouts
salt
freshly grated black pepper

1. Mix together the water, lemon juice and grated lemon rind in a glass or ceramic baking dish.
2. Trim the stems from the Brussels sprouts and remove any brown leaves.
3. Put the sprouts into the dish and roll around to coat with the mixture.
4. Cover and cook in the microwave oven on the highest setting for about five minutes or until the sprouts are just tender. Allow to stand for five minutes, then drain and season to taste with salt and pepper.

Serves 4.

Mustard Greens

¼ lb (125 g) bacon, diced
1 small onion, minced
1 clove garlic, minced
1 lb (500 g) mustard greens, chopped
1 tablespoon chopped chives
salt and pepper

1. Put the bacon in a glass or ceramic casserole dish. Cover the dish with a paper towel and cook in the microwave oven on the highest setting for three minutes.
2. Stir in the onion and garlic and cook, covered, for about three minutes or until the bacon is crisp. Skim off all but about two tablespoons of the bacon fat.
3. Stir the mustard greens and chives into the bacon mixture. Cover and cook for two minutes. Allow to stand for three minutes after removing from the oven.
4. Season to taste with salt and pepper and serve.

Serves 4-6.

Snow Peas

1 lb (500 g) snow peas
¼ cup (65 g) butter
½ teaspoon grated fresh ginger
1 clove garlic, minced
salt and pepper

1. Remove the strings from the peas and rinse in cold water. Drain and set aside.
2. Melt the butter in a glass or ceramic casserole or baking dish, in the microwave oven on the highest setting.
3. Stir in the ginger and garlic and cook for one minute.
4. Add the peas, cover and cook for about six minutes or until the peas are just tender.
5. Season to taste with salt and pepper.

Serves 4-6.

Jerusalem Artichokes

1 lb (500 g) Jerusalem artichokes
¼ cup (65 g) butter
1 tablespoon lemon juice
1 tablespoon minced parsley
salt and pepper

1. Wash the artichokes well then cut in thin slices.
2. Melt the butter in a shallow glass or ceramic baking dish.
3. Stir in the lemon juice.
4. Add the artichokes, cover and cook for about 10-12 minutes or until tender. Stir a few times during the cooking period. Allow to stand for three minutes before serving.
5. Stir in the minced parsley and season to taste with salt and pepper.

Serves 4.

Mushrooms

1 lb (500 g) small fresh mushrooms	⅓ cup sliced scallions
⅓ cup (85 g) butter	salt
1 clove garlic, minced	freshly grated black pepper
1 tablespoon minced fresh basil	minced parsley

1. Wipe the mushrooms with a damp cloth. Cut into thin slices. Set aside.
2. Melt the butter in a glass or ceramic baking dish.
3. Add the garlic and basil and cook in the microwave oven on the highest setting for one minute.
4. Add the mushrooms and mix well. Cover and cook for two minutes, stirring twice during the cooking time.
5. Add the scallions and cook for about five minutes or until the liquid is almost completely evaporated. Stir a few times.
6. Season to taste with salt and pepper and serve garnished with minced parsley.

Serves 4-6.

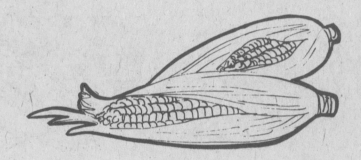

Corn on the Cob (1)

4 ears of corn
butter
salt and pepper

1. Remove the husk and silk from the corn.
2. Wrap the corn in plastic wrap securing the edges well.
3. Put into the microwave oven on the highest setting and cook for about 10-12 minutes or until the corn is tender when pierced.
4. Allow the corn to stand for three minutes before removing the plastic film.
5. Serve with lots of butter, salt and pepper.

Serves 4.

Corn on the Cob (2)

4 ears of corn
butter
salt and pepper

1. Do not remove the husk and silk from the corn. Secure the ends of the husk with string.
2. Cook in the microwave oven for 10-12 minutes or until the corn kernels are tender when pierced through the husk.
3. Remove from the oven and allow to stand for three minutes before removing the husk and silk.
4. Serve with butter, salt and pepper.

Serves 4.

Red Cabbage and Apple

1½ lb (750 g) red cabbage
2 green apples
2 tablespoons (40 ml) melted
butter
1½ tablespoons brown sugar
½ cup (125 ml) red wine vinegar

1. Wash and drain the cabbage. Shred it and pat dry.
2. Peel and core the apples then cut into cubes.
3. Put the cabbage and apples in a glass or ceramic casserole dish and mix in the butter, brown sugar and vinegar.
4. Cover and cook in the microwave oven on the highest setting for 20 minutes, stirring several times during the cooking period.

Serves 6.

Yams

1 lb (500 g) yams
2 tablespoons (40 g) butter
2 tablespoons honey
1 tablespoon lemon juice
½ teaspoon cinnamon

1. Peel the yams. Cut into thick slices.
2. Place the yams in a greased shallow glass baking dish. Cover and cook in the microwave oven for five minutes. Remove from the oven.
3. Combine the butter, honey, lemon juice and cinnamon in a small glass bowl. Heat in the oven for 1½ minutes.
4. Pour the butter mixture over the yams, cover and cook in the oven for one minute. Turn the yams over and reposition in the dish. Cover and cook for two minutes.
5. Remove the cover and baste the yams with the butter mixture. Cook for two minutes or until the yams are tender.

Serves 3-4.

Peppers

4 sweet green or red peppers
1 tablespoon olive oil
1 tablespoon (20 g) butter
1 clove garlic, minced
1 small onion, chopped
salt and pepper

1. Remove the stem and seeds from the peppers. Wash and rinse and cut into thin slices.
2. Heat the olive oil and butter in a shallow glass or ceramic baking dish.
3. Stir in the garlic and onion and cook for one minute.
4. Add the pepper slices, cover and cook for three minutes.
5. Uncover, season to taste with salt and pepper and cook for another two minutes.

Serves 4.

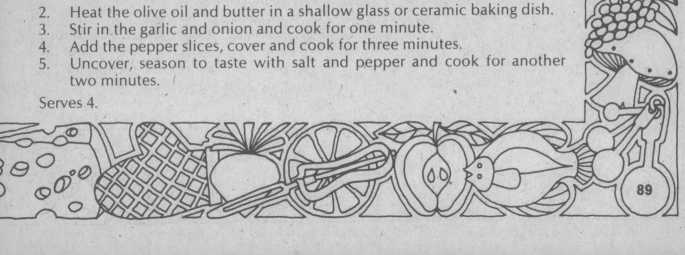

Vegetable Quiche

1 lb (500 g) spinach	½ teaspoon black pepper
3 eggs	1 cup chopped onions
3 egg yolks	1 cup chopped tomatoes
2½ tablespoons flour	1 cup sliced mushrooms
¾ cup (185 ml) milk	¼ cup chopped parsley
¾ cup (185 ml) cream	1 tablespoon (20 g) butter
1 teaspoon salt	sour cream

1. Wash the spinach several times in cold water. Remove the central white stem and chop the spinach coarsely. Put the spinach into an oven bag and seal. Pierce several holes in the top. Cook the spinach in the microwave oven for three minutes or until tender. Drain in a colander pressing out as much liquid as possible.
2. Beat together the eggs and egg yolks in a large bowl.
3. Blend the flour with a little of the milk, then mix with the rest of the milk.
4. Pour the milk and cream into the beaten eggs and mix well. Add the salt and pepper.
5. Fold in the spinach, onions, tomatoes, mushrooms and parsley.
6. Melt the butter in a glass or ceramic pie dish.
7. Pour the quiche mixture into the pie dish and cook in the microwave oven on the highest setting for three minutes. Stir gently. Continue cooking until the quiche is firm — about eight minutes.
8. Remove from the oven and allow to stand for about five minutes before serving.
9. Cut into wedges and serve with a spoonful of sour cream on top of each portion.

Serves 6.

Sweet Potatoes

1 lb (500 g) sweet potatoes
butter
salt
cinnamon or nutmeg

1. Scrub the potatoes well.
2. Prick with a fork in several places.
3. Put the potatoes on a paper towel in the microwave oven and cook for about ten minutes or until tender when pierced.
4. Remove from the oven and allow to stand for five minutes before serving.
5. Serve with butter, salt and cinnamon or nutmeg.

Serves 3-4.

Turnips

1 lb (500 g) turnips
2 tablespoons water
2 tablespoons (40 g) butter
1 clove garlic, minced
salt and pepper
minced chives

1. Wash the turnips and cut into thick slices. Set aside.
2. Put the water, butter and garlic into a glass or ceramic baking dish and heat for one minute, stirring twice during the cooking time.
3. Stir in the turnips, cover and cook for about ten minutes or until the turnips are tender.
4. Allow to stand for three minutes after removing from the oven.
5. Drain well, season to taste with salt and pepper and sprinkle with chives.

Serves 4.

Potatoes au Gratin

2 lb (1 kg) potatoes	1 clove garlic
salt	2 cups grated Swiss cheese
freshly grated black pepper	⅔ cup (165 ml) cream
freshly grated nutmeg or ground nutmeg	2 egg yolks, lightly beaten
	minced chives

1. Peel the potatoes and cut into thin slices.
2. Put a layer of potatoes on a greased shallow glass or ceramic baking dish.
3. Sprinkle on salt, pepper and nutmeg.
4. Mix the garlic with the grated cheese, then sprinkle on about a third of the cheese over the potatoes.
5. Repeat these layers until all the potatoes and cheese are used up, ending with a layer of cheese.
6. Heat the cream in a cup in the microwave oven until it begins to bubble.
7. Slowly add to the egg yolks, stirring constantly. Pour over the potatoes.
8. Cover and cook in the oven for about 20 minutes, turning the dish a quarter of a turn every five minutes. When the potatoes are tender, remove from the oven and allow to stand for five minutes before serving.
9. Serve garnished with minced chives.

Serves 6-8.

Baked Potatoes

4 medium potatoes
salt and pepper
butter
sour cream
chives

1. Scrub the potatoes very well.
2. Prick with a fork in several places.
3. Put on a paper towel in the microwave oven and cook for about 20 minutes or until the potatoes are soft when pierced.
4. Remove from the oven and allow to stand for five minutes before serving.
5. Serve with salt and pepper, butter, sour cream and chives.

Serves 4.

Carrots

1 lb (500 g) small tender carrots
2 tablespoons (40 g) butter
2 tablespoons honey
salt and pepper

1. Top and tail the carrots. If very young and tender, do not peel.
2. Place the carrots in an oven bag and seal the bag. Pierce several holes in the top of the bag.
3. Cook in the microwave oven on the highest setting for about seven minutes or until tender. Allow to stand for five minutes after removing from the oven.
4. Put the carrots (sliced, if you like) into a glass or ceramic serving dish. Put on the butter, honey and salt and pepper to taste. Mix well and heat through in the oven.

Serves 4.

Cauliflower

1 medium cauliflower, whole
2 tablespoons water
¼ cup (65 ml) melted butter
salt
black pepper
paprika

1. Trim leaves and core from the cauliflower. Put the cauliflower whole into an oven bag. Sprinkle on the two tablespoons of water and seal the bag. Pierce several holes in the top of the bag to allow steam to escape.
2. Cook in the microwave oven on the highest setting for about ten minutes or until the cauliflower is tender.
3. Allow to stand for five minutes after removing from the oven.
4. Put the cauliflower on a heated serving dish and pour on the melted butter. Season to taste with salt and pepper and sprinkle with paprika.

Serves 6.

General Hints

Microwave Cooking

COOKING TIME:

The quantity of food in the oven will affect the length of cooking time. The more food, the longer it will take.

Cold food will take longer to cook than food at room temperature.

Food continues to cook after being removed from the oven. Allow for this when calculating the length of cooking time.

UTENSILS:

You may use glass, ceramic, paper and woven baskets to cook in.

DO NOT use any metal containers or even pottery with silver or gold trim. Metal reflects the microwaves and can cause irreparable damage to the oven.

Plastic food wrap can be used to cover baking dishes or casserole dishes.

Although microwave ovens are safe and the manufacture of them is regulated by the National Electrical Manufacturers Association, it is a good idea to have the leakage checked at regular intervals.

N.B. It is most important that your microwave oven be used in accordance with the manufacturer's instructions. Since all microwave ovens vary, be sure to read these instructions regarding temperature and general use before cooking.

Index

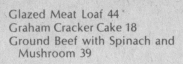